TALK TO
YOUR PLANTS

TALK TO YOUR PLANTS

and other gardening know-how I learned from Grandma Putt

by
Jerry Baker

Literary Consultant: Dan Kibbie

Nash Publishing, Los Angeles

ALSO BY JERRY BAKER:

Plants Are Like People
Jerry Baker's Back to Nature Almanac

To Ilene, my beautiful and loving wife,
and to my children,
Sue, Diane, Pat and Jeff

Contents

Introduction

Once, when I was about ten years old, my mother and father let me spend a whole school year and the following summer vacation at my Grandma Puttnam's.

My Grandma had a way with youngsters, and as soon as my family had left to go back into town, she took me for a walk in her fantastic garden and introduced me to her friends. It never seemed even a little odd to me, at the time, that Grandma treated her plants just like people, or that she would spend long hours conversing with them. She never seemed to feel the slightest bit awkward about including her city-bred grandson in those conversations. And, it wasn't many days before I was wandering around the place, jabbering away to "Grandpa Putt," the big horse chestnut out front by the road, and to "Great Grandpa Coolidge," the old maple tree near the back porch. My favorite was a huge white oak way back at the edge of her property which Grandma and I named "Chief Black Feathers." I would lie on my back and look up at the branches and start talking. Before long, I could see the Old Chief take form in the thousands of leaves shimmering black against the sunlight.

Grandma Putt was a remarkable woman—a real honest-to-goodness pioneer. As a small girl, she had helped Great-Grandpa Coolidge carve their farm right out of the Indian Territory. She was part Indian herself, and she treated each plant, tree and flower as an individual with a spirit and personality of its own. She taught me how to recognize these plant peculiarities and personality traits and ways to use them to make a successful garden. The plants in her garden were her friends. She looked out for them, and they looked out for her.

For miles around, she was renowned as the local gardening expert. She won so many ribbons for her flowers and vegetables at the County Fair that, sometimes, the judges would ask her not to enter a particular competition so they would be able to encourage other gardeners with a chance at the prizes.

People would come to her from all over with sick house plants, diseased patches of grass, weeds they wanted identified, and a multitude of questions about an enormous variety of gardening problems and projects.

Grandma never charged for her good advice or home remedies. As often as not, she would send the supplicant away with new hope and a basket of berries or fresh vegetables, or what she called "pantry herbs."

My Grandma didn't believe it was right for a boy my age to have too much idle time on his hands, so she assigned me a whole list of "character building" chores taking care of her "plant people." She said that if I talked to the plants, and listened to what they had to tell me, I would be able to develop a green thumb.

That was a time in my life when I was convinced that my Grandma Putt knew just about everything. Most of her knowledge came from hard work and experience. Some of it was handed down from her Indian and pioneer ancestors. I don't remember ever seeing her read any books except her time-worn Bible and her almanacs. But, somehow, somewhere, she had accumulated an amazing amount of information on the art, history, lore, and science of gardening. To tell the truth, I learned a lot more from her about gardening that summer than I have learned in all the years since.

Over the years, I have attempted to add to that storehouse of gardening know-how that Grandma Putt left with me. I have tried to keep up with my reading on the subject and with most of the new products, tools and techniques. Time and time again, I have discovered that Grandma's old-fashioned methods are really the modern methods; that some of the "newest" discoveries, were techniques that she had used effectively more than forty years ago!

Of course, there have been some revolutionary break-throughs in the past two or three decades that have made certain aspects of home gardening safe, easier and less time-consuming. Only the most hardened "organic fanatic" would disregard or belittle these advances.

But, over all the years that organic and chemical gardeners have been feuding, I have found that Grandma Putt's commonsense methods have worked best. They have been tested and found successful by five generations of my family.

I intend to present those commonsense methods in this book. Some of the anecdotes, techniques and remedies you will find in the chapters ahead are very old-fashioned. Others, have to do with new methods, instructions, tools and products that seem to work and make good sense.

I believe that it will take a mixture of old and new ideas to make our country, our families, and our gardens great. I hope that I have included in these pages a good part of the knowledge and pleasure that I gained from gardening with Grandma.

Chapter 1.
Getting Acquainted
with
Mother Earth

For a ten-year-old boy, coming to the country in June is like a leap to another universe. The month starts right off with a good beginning by presenting you with the last day of school. Then, unlike April or May which are nice but can't quite be trusted, June offers the whole outdoors complete with sunshine. If it does rain on a ten-year-old, something that doesn't seem possible from this perspective, who cares! For me, at ten, the countryside, outdoors and June were three stars in a perfect constellation!

Spending the summer at Grandma Putt's offered added excitement, because I figured I would pretty much have the run of the world. The world was an unpaved road that ran past her house, over a wooden bridge at the creek and on through the woods. In the other direction, the world ended on the north side of a little town where we would go almost every day for shopping and delivering eggs or dropping off some flowers or vegetables to someone who couldn't be up and about. In those days, they called that "bein' neighborly."

On the north side of town was a park where they showed free movies outdoors every Friday night. Beyond that, were the railroad tracks where bad kids my age would play doctor or smoke in the boxcars parked at the siding. Down the tracks, was the grainery owned by Mr. Hodges who was also the director of the bank. There was Evans's nursery and Lovers' Lane on that side of town too. High-school kids parked up there on date nights. During the day it didn't look like much. There was a train trestle which we kids dared each other to cross with our eyes closed and some buffalo wallows. Although I'm sure that no one, not even Grandma Putt, ever saw a buffalo wallow there. The whole area had once been part of a military tract set aside for the Indians. Even then, a hundred years later, I could sometimes find arrowheads in the creek or along its banks where the Indians had camped. I was very much into Indians in those days and I considered it a shame that I had been born so late that I missed all the buffalo-hunting and scalp-taking. Grandma Puttnam knew all about those things, and for that reason she seemed especially blessed.

Her house was very big and very old, the kind of big rambling farmhouse that is so typical of the early Midwest you get the feeling that they were sold by the Monkey Ward's catalogue. The big trees out front were spaced far enough apart to give folks on the road a good view of Grandma's big front yard and the house. A large snowball bush was all that separated passersby from the front porch, which was high, wide and gray, and filled with well-used old rockers and a hanging swing. Sometimes the chickens or geese would get under it to lay eggs. If we didn't check every once in a while, the eggs would rot. Then it would be a couple of days before the grownups would sit out again.

Sitting out in the evenings was the big thing for the older folks. We kids would play hide-and-seek or we would catch fireflies and put them in jars to make lanterns, but the oldsters would just sit for hours and talk. They had two or three favorite spots. The front porch, the wooden lawn chairs near the arbor leading to the rose garden, and out back. While we kids would sit in the cold cellar and tell ghost stories, they would sit for hours and talk about Lord knows what; everything, from gardening to gossip, I guess.

4

That was before TV, when porches were used for sitting and families talked with one another about all sorts of things. If we were lucky, Grandma Putt would tell about living with the Indians or Grandpa Puttnam, if he was home, would talk about his horses. He was a horse trader and trainer. Next to Grandma, horses were the passion of his life. He raised trotters and pacers and during the summer he took them out on the County Fair circuit.

I was looking forward to all of this summer fun when Grandma Putt came up with an idea that dashed my hopes and changed my life.

We had gone to town and, after shopping at the Royal Blue, we stopped at Reed's Hotel to buy me an ice-cream cone. I liked their cones best because they had little slips of paper at the bottom with the name of the cone company on them. If the slip said FREE, old man Reed gave you a free ice-cream cone. It was always a temptation to bite off the bottom of the cone right away to see if you were lucky. Anyway, we were walking along main street with me fighting temptation, and all of a sudden Grandma jolted me out of my reverie.

"Junior, I think it's about time we lay out some jobs for you to do this summer. A little work is the best thing for a boy your age."

Work! The word had a nasty ring that reminded me of living at home in the city. Work was something like taking out the garbage, or shoveling the snow off the driveway just when your favorite radio program happened to be on. Work was no fun. I was musing over these horrors as she continued.

"Yes, it's about time you got acquainted with Mother Earth. No sense in wasting a good growing season like this just rambling around. Tomorrow you can get started planning for your Victory garden."

A Victory garden? Well, that wasn't as bad as I had

thought it was going to be. There was something attractive and manly about growing a garden. Besides, it was outside.

World War II was in progress at the time, and everyone was very patriotic. I had been doing my part by smashing tin cans, saving tinfoil, and collecting bubble-gum cards commemorating the Dieppe Raid and the Battle of Midway, but now, I was being given the opportunity to take on more responsibility and plant a Victory garden! There was a community V-garden in town already, and everyone was asked to give a little of their time to help make it grow. Now, some people were setting aside part of their own land for Victory gardens of their own. The idea seemed commendable to me. Not quite as exciting as grenading Nazis or Nips, but better than a city paper drive. It was easy to picture whole regiments enjoying my corn and beans. I couldn't wait to get back home and begin!

When we got home, Grandma took me out behind the tool shed where the vegetable garden was planted every year. There were rows of radishes, lettuce, beets and carrots showing crisp and green and leafy against the brown loamy soil. Tomato seedlings were in flats, ready for transplanting; peas and beans and potatoes had been put in the ground and, except for the last, were marked out by the envelopes of the seed packets tacked to sticks at the end of each row.

I remember thinking that if a little old lady like my Grandma could grow a garden that looked this good—just wait and see what a strong healthy boy like me could do. It would be great! I could see my garden already, in my imagination, stretched out for acres until it blurred against a distant horizon.

"Junior, you'd better go to the house and get your notebook and a pencil. And you'd better bring that big ball of string in the left-hand drawer by the kitchen counter." Quickly, I was gone and back.

6

"Now, let's lay out your garden over there." She pointed to a weedy patch of ground just beyond her garden.

"Not nearly large enough for me," I thought.

"That was the garden, year before last. Of course you won't want to use all that ground for your first garden. It's better to start small, with something you can handle."

Was she kidding? I knew I could handle a garden four times that size. "I'll probably have to cut down a couple of those trees and clear some of those bramble berries over there, so's I can extend this little plot," I bragged to myself.

"All right boy, take your string and some of these sticks and stake out this plot. Figure on twenty rows ten feet long, with a foot in-between rows."

I was mortified. Such a tiny garden! "Oh well," I shrugged, "I'll start small and do such a good job, she'll want me to double it in no time." Already those regiments had grown. By then, my Victory garden was feeding the entire African invasion force!

Planning Your First Garden

Today, when I read most gardening books and articles that give instructions for laying out a vegetable garden, I can't help but remember how foolhardy I had been about planning that first Victory garden with Grandma Putt. The books and articles all recommend starting with hundred-foot rows! My recommendations are much more modest. If you are a semi-experienced gardener, plan for twenty-five-foot rows. But if you're a beginner, plan on ten-foot rows. Planning a garden is like ordering food at a restaurant: Don't let your eyes be bigger than your stomach. Grandma knew that short rows that receive the proper care and attention will produce as much as long rows you can't handle.

"When you plan a garden," she said, "be sure it's of a size you can *do well*. Because if you show Mother Earth that you're earnest and willing to work, she'll reward you with a harvest of plenty." She said one of her almanacs quoted Henry Ward Beecher as saying, "A *half* well done is better than a *whole* half done."

Make a Plan and Stick To It

Grandma said that before anyone starts to plan his garden, he should decide what kind of a gardener he wants to be that year. She said there are three kinds of gardeners: those who garden for the fun of it, those who garden for work (cash crops), and those who garden for the fun of work. If you haven't raised herbs, flowers or vegetables before, and don't need to sell what you raise, start out small so the job doesn't become too grueling and turn you off gardening altogether; if you have the time, the muscles, and the patience (and a little experience) and want to give or sell some of your produce, plant a middle-sized garden; and, if, in the words of Mr. Rodale, you are looking for "pay dirt," plan a large enough plot to meet those ends.

Where to Put Your Garden

I don't want you to get the idea that Grandma Putt hid her garden out behind the tool shed so that people wouldn't see it. On the contrary, her vegetable garden was in plain view of her back porch. I think she liked to sit out there on nice evenings in the spring and summer and watch her friends grow.

8

Actually, all of Grandma's place was a garden. Her asparagus and stocks grew, mixed together and wild, along the stone fence down by the road. The soil there was sandy and the asparagus thrived with very little attention paid to it. Rhubarb, or "pie plant" as she called it, sometimes, came up every year in a small patch by the well, mixed in with some calla lilies. Behind the calla lilies were four rows of grape arbors. There were pantry herbs mixed in with the flower beds below the kitchen window. There was garlic and onion growing with the roses. What I am saying is, don't hide your garden. Looking at it, talking to it and having company share its success stories will be one of your most enjoyable pastimes.

If you have ever seen me on television, or read *Plants Are Like People,* you probably know that I am a strong advocate of using your landscaping space to grow plants that will pay their way. Why not have food and flowers as well as foliage? It was Grandma Putt who taught me that strawberries and squash can make attractive groundcovers. They will also provide the fare for some very tasty meals. When you have to disguise an object or location, always check over your list of favorite fruits, nuts, berries or vegetables and, more than likely, you will find something that will fill the bill.

It was from the English that we learned the custom of mixing flowers with the vegetables in the kitchen garden. Today, many of my suburban and city-dwelling friends do the British one better by using lettuce and flowers for a border along walks and at the side of their houses. They put tomatoes next to their evergreens on a sunny side of the house, and climbing beans with the sweetpeas on the side of the garage. Some apartment dwellers even grow radishes, carrots, tomatoes, onions, lettuce, and potatoes in tubs and window boxes on their tiny balconies. If you don't have a lot of room, you don't have to give up on the idea of having a vegetable garden. It may not end up looking like one you see pictured in the gardening books, but if you take advantage of the space you do have available, it can be just as productive.

Here are some of the important factors to consider when you are looking for a spot to raise most vegetables.

Full Sun

Sunlight is the first consideration in deciding on the placement of your vegetables since most vegetables need six to eight hours of sunlight a day if they are to do a good productive job for you. The best time to look for a spot is early in the morning, when you will be able to tell whether your location will get the warmth of the early morning sun. If your garden is one of the first places to warm up during the day, it will also be one of the first places to have warm soil in the spring.

Some leafy vegetables can take more shade than potatoes, tomatoes or corn. So, it's okay to put cabbage, lettuce, broccoli, beans, spinach and chard where they might get a little respite from Old Sol during the hottest parts of the day.

Get Rid of the Sod Over Your Vegetable Patch

If you are going to plant your garden where sod is now growing, take the sod off and use it to fill in bare spots in your lawn, or put it on your compost pile. Too many gardeners try to turn the sod under. This often results in getting grass and weed seeds up to the surface where they can germinate and be a troublesome bother when you really want to spend your time growing vegetables instead of weeding.

In the Beginning, Your Garden Needs Weeds

I think I mentioned that the area that Grandma Putt pointed out to me as a good location for my Victory garden was full of weeds. When I asked her about this, she said that weeds indicate good soil fertility. It's when nothing much is growing in a given area that you should think twice before planting something there. Generally speaking, the thicker the weed cover, the better the fertility in the soil below.

Someone once said, "A man doesn't know anything about life unless he puts his own two hands in the dirt and makes something grow." I agree wholeheartedly with this statement, but I take exception to one word in it. That word is *dirt*. To me, there is a big difference between plain old dirt and good garden soil.

A spade full of good soil is an amazing world full of a staggering number of living things and a complex amount of organic and mineral substances. Grandma Putt called it, "Mother Earth's Boarding House." Any soil scientist will tell you it's pretty difficult to generalize about soils. The soil on your land may be completely different from your neighbor's.

Unfortunately, not all soil is good soil for growing. Good soil is dirt in which ingredients and conditions for fertility (conditions in which plant reproduction and growth can take place) are added. These ingredients and conditions are: good drainage, good structure, presence and availability of proper nutrients, a proper balance between acidity and alkalinity, good aeration, the ability to hold up to 40% of its own total content in moisture, and the proper temperature.

Back in the old days when people were close to the earth, farmers and gardeners played their soil conditions pretty much by ear. They would spread on a layer of manure every year and toss on a few shovelfuls of lime whenever they thought the soil was getting "sour." Nowadays, most of us have been separated from the good earth so long we don't have this instinctive feel for what we are doing. So, if your soil instincts are dull, here's what to do.

Good Drainage

After sunlight, the next important prerequisite that Grandma said we needed for our garden location was good drainage.

"People who want to garden," she said, "have got to learn to think perpendicular. Begin to think about what's going on under the ground, instead of concentrating on the half of your garden that sticks out here in the air."

Grandma Putt had gardened in my Victory garden spot before, so she knew that the drainage was excellent. If you are uncertain about the drainage under a location you intend to use, check it before you begin.

THE OLD-FASHIONED RAINBARREL TEST

You can check the drainage by using the old-fashioned rainbarrel test. That is, if you happen to have an old-fashioned rainbarrel. Not too long ago, everybody kept a big thirty- or fifty-gallon barrel at some convenient outside location to catch rainwater. I'm really surprised that all the ladies who are antique collectors haven't discovered that old custom and brought it back as a fad. Water from rain or snow is the best thing for your plant friends because of the high amounts of nitrogen it contains. It's really terrific for houseplants and washing your hair. Anyway, here's how to use the rainbarrel to test the drainage in your garden plot. Put the barrel in the center of the garden area and fill it with the garden hose. Then, tip the barrel over and watch to see how quickly the water runs off. If there are still large puddles after a half hour or so, you have some drainage problems; and if the water disappears almost immediately, that also means trouble.

WHAT CAUSES POOR DRAINAGE

If the water puddles up and stands in spots, you probably have too much clay in your soil or, in some parts of the country, you may possibly have a layer of hardpan under the topsoil. Hardpan is an impervious shell-like layer that must be broken up if you are going to have good drainage and good root growth. If hardpan is a huge problem, instead of just occurring in isolated spots, you may have to dig down to it and lay grain tile. If you don't want to do all that work, move your garden!

On the other hand, if the barrel of water disappears very quickly, your soil is too sandy. Sandy soils won't hold much moisture. Water runs through them as fast as it does off a duck's back.

How Does Your Soil Structure Stack Up?

United States Department of Agriculture soil experts advise that you can check the structure of your soil this way. Take a large glass jar, at least a quart in size. Into it, put two cups of water and a cup of your soil. Shake it thoroughly and let it settle. Then shake it up again and let it settle for about a week to ten days, or until the water in the jar becomes clear again. Now, look at the way your soil has settled in the jar.

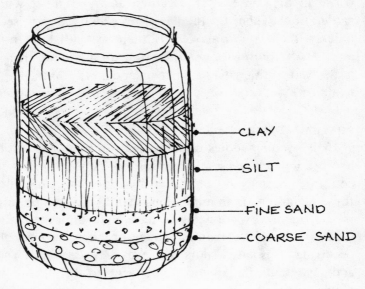

CLAY
SILT
FINE SAND
COARSE SAND

GOOD SANDY LOAM

If the soil is what it should be . . . fine sandy loam, it will have layered out in the following proportions. The bottom layer will be sand with the coarser sand at the bottom and the fine sand just above it. This sand layer should make up about two-fifths of the soil in the jar. The next layer will be silt. This layer should make up the second two-fifths of the soil in the jar. The top layer of soil will be clay. This layer should comprise one-fifth of the total soil content. If your soil stacks up this way, you have a *good sandy loam.*

LIGHT SOILS

Soils that contain too much sand are called *light soils.* They are easy to work, usually warm up first in the spring, but are often unable to hold enough moisture for growing plants.

14

HEAVY OR CLAY SOILS

Soils that contain too much silt or clay are called *heavy* or *clay* soils. These either retain too much moisture, or will not accept moisture because of the limited space between the soil particles. These heavy soils have a tendency to stay cold and soggy too late into the spring planting season. Once you try spading up a plot of clay soil, you'll understand why it's called *heavy soil!*

ANOTHER VITAL SOIL INGREDIENT: HUMUS

When you make your soil test with the quart jar containing a cup of water and a cup of your soil, you will probably see some material floating on the top after the soil has settled and the water has cleared. This floating debris is *humus.* The good loam that I mentioned before contains a proper balance of sand, silt and clay. It also contains plenty of humus.

Humus is a dark brown or black substance that is the residue of decayed or decaying organic matter. That is to say it is made up of either plant or animal matter, including bacteria and fungi, that have been returned to the soil. Humus is essential for supplying the soil with nutrients, texture and the ability to hold moisture.

In nature, snow and rain are the keys to working humus into the soil. But in your garden, you can add these life-giving organic substances yourself.

How to Correct Soil-Drainage and Structure Problems

As you can see, good drainage and good soil structure are closely tied together. If you have a drainage problem because your soil is too light or too heavy, here's how to correct it.

15

What to do with Light, Sandy Soil

To improve light-sand soil, mix in plenty of compost, peat moss, leaf-mold, wood by-products (bark, chips, and sawdust) or green manure. I have listed these in their order of effectiveness. Another soil-building technique to use when you're not rushed for time is to plant a cover crop of cereal rye. Do this in the early fall. Then when it comes up after a few weeks, plow it under. The organic matter which this heavy-rooted crop contains will break down by spring and you'll be ready to go. Farmers have been using cover crops of cereal rye and clover for years. Clover returns lots of nitrogen to the soil as do all the legumous plants.

What to Do With Heavy Silt, or Clay Soils

To improve heavy silt or clay soils, add gypsum, wood chips, compost, peat moss, or leaf-mold. If there is an over-abundance of clay, add perlite, vermiculite, or sand. However, you can use up an awful lot of sand even in a small garden area. Don't add sand unless absolutely necessary. And, if you live along the seacoast, don't add shore sand unless you wash it thoroughly many many times. Ocean beach sand contains high concentrations of salt which will kill most plants. Plants are like people; you can't take ocean sand or water. Neither can your plants.

Organic Substances that Add Humus to Your Soil

If you were going to ask a friend or neighbor to give you something, or put himself out for you in some way, you would probably be inclined to give him a little "present" for his kind efforts. Well, before you ask Mother Earth to take care of a bunch of baby vegetables, it might be wise to surprise her with a little present. The nicest gift you can give her, and all the bacteria and microorganisms she has staying in her boardinghouse, is humus. To add humus to your soil you might want to experiment with one or more of the following additives.

GREEN MANURE

Green manure is best applied during the fall of the year. It takes two forms; cover crops and plant debris.

Cover cropping has been practiced by farmers for centuries. Plant a crop of cereal rye or clover early in the fall. Plow deeply when you plant. Be sure to turn up a good eighteen inches of soil. Then, when the crop comes up in a few weeks, plow it under. Over the winter, your soil will decompose the green plant material and the roots. Then, in spring, it will be ready to go and ready to grow! Cereal rye is good because it develops an enormous root system. Clover is also good; it is a legume and contains large amounts of nitrogen which it will return to the soil.

If you don't want to try cover cropping, just take any plant debris—grass clippings, old pea plants, leaves, sawdust, woodchips, etc.—work it into your soil in the fall. You can use garbage, too. By spring, this will have broken down into humus. The grass, pea plants, and bean plants will also return a great deal of nitrogen.

COMPOST

As any organic gardener will tell you at the drop of a blade of grass (on his compost heap), compost is the best humus-building additive you can give your soil.

The difference between compost and green manure is that with compost you lay your grass clippings and other organic refuse in a heap, and let the decomposition take place above-ground before you mix it into your garden soil. There are at least a hundred ways to make a compost pile. Many of the old-timers usually had two going at once: one that was ready for spreading and one that was "working." You can use just about any material in your compost heap just as long as you keep turning it often enough to let the airborne bacteria get at it. These bacteria will not only help with the decomposition, they will eliminate a lot of the odors.

Some typical compost ingredients are:

Animal wastes from horses, cows, chickens, goats, sheep, pigs, pigeons, geese, ducks and human night soil. This includes sweeping from stalls and coops and pens where such animals are kept. Garbage such as eggshells, meat scraps and small bones are also fine.

Plant debris from grass cuttings, fallen leaves, prunings, stalks of peas, beans, or corn, lettuce leaves, stock from boiling vegetables, peelings, coffee grounds, popcorn, faded flower cuttings and, even, weeds. Grandma and other old-timers put in pet herbs and weeds like yarrow, dandelion, and chamomile. She said they were the wonder-workers of her compost heap.

Earths like sod turf, topsoil, river soil and peat or sewage sludge.

Be careful about putting any large items suffering from plant disease on your compost heap, they might not decompose. Also, don't put anything greasy on it. Where you locate your compost heap has a lot to do with where your garden is and where your neighbors are. Try to keep it as close to your garden as possible; at the same time, if prevailing winds threaten to blow compost odors your way or toward your neighbors, either locate it elsewhere or feed it materials that don't tend to putrefy. You can do much to ward off putrefaction by just turning the heap every ten days or so.

As I said, there are lots of ways to build a compost heap. Here is Grandma Putt's sure-fire compost recipe.

Find your spot. Dig up the sod and turn it over. Wet it slightly. This bottom layer should be approximately half a foot to ten inches high. Now, put down a layer of old newspapers and wet it until soggy. Next, put on a thin layer of animal waste, more wet newspaper, plant waste, newspaper, topsoil. Keep rotating, animal-newspaper-plant-topsoil layers until you build your heap up to about four feet. Each layer should be no more than three or four inches thick. Keep the pile moist not soggy—about the wetness of a load of wash that has had most of the moisture spun out in the washer.

Turn your compost heap every ten days to two weeks. At least three times during a season.

The square footage of your compost heap depends on how big a garden you are planning and how much material you have available to compost. Even a small pile can bring lots of good humus to your soil.

Many people don't think about making a compost heap until the fall of the year. If they would start in spring, saving their grass clippings, spent bean and pea plants, etc., they could really do their garden a favor and practice ecology at the same time.

OTHER HUMUS-BUILDING ADDITIVES

There are organic soil additives other than compost and green manure which may work very well to improve the structure and texture of your specific soil. Here is a list of those most commonly available on the commercial market.

> bark
> lignified wood
> manure
> oak-leaf mold
> peat mosses (hypnum, sedge, and spagnum)
> redwood products
> sawdust

The Presence and Availability of Nutrients in Your Soil

Lots of folks get confused and decide that soil nutrients are taken in as food by the plants in their garden. That is not precisely true. Nutrients are the minerals and chemicals the plants need to manufacture their own food.

If you want to grow a healthy patch of vegetables, a certain amount of minerals must be present in the soil. The most important are nitrogen, phosphorus, and potash or potassium.

Nitrogen encourages leafy growth and succulence. It is supplied by rain and snow but your garden will need additional applications by you. Your soil has the ability to hold some nitrogen in the form of humus.

Phosphorus promotes the development of the root system of your plants. It also helps the plant mature quickly. Most vegetables require large amounts of phosphorus. Your soil doesn't hold phosphorus very well; that's why you'll need to choose a fertilizer that has a high phosphorus content.

Potash helps build fibrous tissues and is necessary for the manufacture of starches and sugars. In sandy soils, a higher amount of potash is needed in your fertilizer.

Trace elements are also vitally necessary to promote healthful plant reproduction and growth. Among those needed most are boron, calcium, chlorine, copper, iron, manganese, sodium, sulphur, and zinc.

The Acid/Alkaline Teeter-Totter

It isn't enough that all these mineral elements be present in the soil. In order to be able to help the plants grow, the nutrients must be available on demand of the plant roots. Sometimes, too much acidity or alkalinity in the soils inhibits mineral availability. Grandma Putt used to pay close attention to her plants. If she spotted a yellowing of new young leaves, she knew the soil was not making iron available. Alkaline soil withholds iron and other nutrients. So Grandma would just mix a little lime into the soil to "sweeten" it.

You can test the balance between acids and alkalines in your soil by a very simple test which your USDA area station will be happy to do at a very minimal fee. This test will check what is known as the pH content of the soil.

PH Content

PH means potential of hydrogen. It is measured on a scale from 0 to 14 with 7 as the midway, or neutral point. If your

21

soil tests out seven or above, it is on the alkaline side. Most vegetables require slightly acid, but not too acid, soil.

The closer you keep your soil to neutral pH, the better it will be for your plants. Write or call your Ag station for a bulletin telling how to extract a soil sample for them to check.

Correcting "Sweet" and "Sour" Soil

If your soil checks out on the acid side, you may want to add lime to sweeten it. The amount of lime you will need to apply will be suggested by the Ag station or lab that does your test. A general application consists of 50 pounds of lime to each 1,000 square feet of garden or lawn. You can use agricultural lime and apply it with a spreader, or you can take a tip from the old-timers and apply hydrated lime, that is, lime suspended in water. Another soil "sweetener" used by Grandma and her friends was plain old wood ashes from their fireplaces. If you live on the seacoast, ground shells contain lime and are available at local garden centers.

If your soil shows too much alkalinity, you will want to make it more acid. Good old Garden Prize Gypsum will do the trick. The gypsum should be applied in a fairly thin layer. Figure on using about 35 pounds of gypsum for each 1,000 square feet of garden space. Other acid-adding ingredients which you might have handy are: beech or oak sawdust and sulphur. Add about a gallon of powdered sulphur to each 1,000 square feet of soil. If you live in the mountains, like my friends Dan and Mary Kibbie, don't throw away those bushels and bushels of pine needles that are constantly showering down from the cedars, Douglas firs, and the redwoods. Pine needles contain acid. By the way, they also make an excellent mulch.

Aeration Is Half the Battle

Grandma Putt said that when she was a young girl, farmers who worked just the top six or ten inches of their soil were mocked, and called fools or lazybones behind their backs.

She said when she checked, sure enough, the fellows who ploughed shallow had the worst-looking farms and the poorest yields at harvest. While the farmers who ploughed deep had the best-looking and most productive farms.

"Plough deep in the fall and shallow in the spring." That was the rule of the successful farmers of the eighteenth and nineteenth centuries.

What does all this have to do with aeration? Why everything! Your soil should be worked to a depth of eighteen inches in the fall or winter (if you live out west). This creates lots of passageways for the air to filter down to the subsoil level. This air will supply the roots of your plants with oxygen and nitrogen in amounts critical to the plants' well-being.

The amount of pore space needed for good plant growth should be about equal to the amount of solid material.

When the winter is over, soil ploughed in the fall will be easier to work in the spring. It will get more air and, thus, warm up and dry out more quickly.

Don't think you can do this deep ploughing in the spring. If you do, you will get good aeration, but you will also bring inferior and infertile subsoil up at the wrong time and put it in contact with your plant babies.

Your Soil's Ability to Catch and Hold Moisture

Nothing goes on in the world of plants without water. Water is the only medium in which all the chemical processes so essential to plant life and plant growth can take place.

23

Grandma Putt told me that plants use water like our bodies use blood. She said that the difference is that plants are continually losing water vapor from the leaf surfaces, so they need to replenish what is lost by obtaining a new supply from the soil through the root system. The root hairs on most plants are able to absorb incredibly tiny amounts of moisture from the thin film of water that surrounds each particle of soil.

Plant scientists say that the conditions in which plants grow best allow the soil to catch and hold up to forty percent of its own content in moisture. By creating the proper soil structure and texture with additives, and by aerating your soil, you will be able to prepare a garden or lawn seedbed with the moisture-holding capacity so necessary to your "plant people."

Temperature

All too often, inexperienced gardeners fail to take the temperature into account when they begin to plant. Grandma said that in order to grow vegetables, it's important to have a good idea of the temperature of the soil and of the air above the soil.

None of us can control the weather, and no weatherman can predict accurately enough to give any guarantee of exactly when planting should begin. Many farmers and gardeners rush to get everything in the ground as soon as the last frost of the spring has passed. However, there is a definite lag period between the last spring frost and the day when the sun has warmed your soil to a "growing temperature."

Many helpful microorganisms and soil bacteria are immobile if the soil is too cold. They become very much more

24

active as the soil temperature rises into the sixties and the seventies.

Light sandy soil warms quickly, while heavy clay soil remains cold and soggy sometimes well into May or even June, depending on current local conditions. The growing season in some parts of Maine, Minnesota, and other states along the Canadian border doesn't begin until after mid-June, and ends as early as the first of September.

Perennials like asparagus, artichokes and rhubarb, and root or leafy vegetables, are traditionally planted in early spring because they can germinate and grow in cooler soils.

Grandma said that the temperature at *night* is more important to us gardeners than day temperatures. She said that years of experience and experimenting had proved to her that many vegetables, like corn, tomatoes, potatoes, beets, turnips, and sweet potatoes, "set" their crops at night. When I asked her why that happens, she said it was one of many mysteries that take place in a garden. Another unsolved mystery is why each plant "sets" best within a certain specific temperature range. She said that a summer with cool nights will be better for potato crops than for tomatoes. She said that's why Maine and Idaho have always been such good potato-growing states. When planning your garden, check to see if certain plants have a tradition of growing well in your local temperature conditions. It's all right to experiment with new plants, but check first to see if they grow well in similar climatic conditions before you invest very much money in them. Time, experience, and accurate record-keeping will teach you a great deal about the temperatures needed for proper plant nourishment and growth. Since this is the one important factor of your soils' productiveness that you have no control over, you will have to be particularly observant and adaptable to Mother Earth's local timetable. If the spring is cold and wet, delay planting until the warm sunny days begin. Plantings put down in too cold soil will only wait for these warm days before they start to grow. There is no "getting the jump" on Mother Earth.

Getting "a feel for" the soil in my garden and learning not to rush the "natural ways of things" were two important lessons that have stuck with me from that year when Grandma first introduced me to Mother Earth.

Chapter 2.
The Victorious
Victory Gardener

There are bushels and bushels of good reasons why you and your family should go into vegetable gardening. The least important of these may be the satisfaction you and your taste buds will feel when you sit down to a meal which includes a colorful variety of taste-pleasing vegetables you grew yourself.

As the seasons I spend in my garden turn into years, and the years pass—all too swiftly—I have come to understand that it is crucial for all of us—especially our children—to reestablish and reaffirm our fragile interdependence with all the living and growing things on God's green earth.

Many more important books than this, and many more important thinkers than I, have eloquently delivered the urgent warning that we are dangerously close to upsetting the ecological balance forever.

Almost a decade ago, Adlai Stevenson suggested that we begin to think of our earth as a giant spaceship hurtling toward the stars and the next century carrying billions of passengers with a limited life-support system. Governor Stevenson saw that we "spacemen" must be extremely careful not to foul up the air and water supply or crowd out the animals and plant life which are all so vitally necessary to make our "earth-ship" livable, so that the generations who come after us will be able to fly her into the future.

My Grandma Putt might not have been turned on by this eminent citizen of the world's analogy about space and spaceships. But she would have known what he meant immediately if she could have seen him walking the fields of his farm at Libertyville, Illinois.

She once told me that farmers and gardeners just seem to understand instinctively that we are only stewards of the land. That, somehow, by touching Mother Earth and working with her, we realize that it is up to each of us to take good care of her, passing her on to our sons and daughters in better shape than she was when we received her.

She said that this concept of good stewardship and responsibility for the land is an important lesson that she learned from her Bible and her Indian upbringing.

> And the Lord God took man, and put him in the garden of Eden to dress it and keep it.
>
> Genesis 2:3-15.

The great English scholar, Sir Francis Bacon was not the first, nor was my humble Grandmother Puttnam the last gardener to read a special meaning in the Book of Genesis. In the nineteenth century, Sir William Temple wrote:

> If we believe in the scripture, we must allow that God Almighty esteemed the life of man in a garden the happiest he could give him, or else He would not have placed Adam in that of Eden.

Grandma felt that most conservation-minded Bible readers get confused when they read in Genesis 1:28 that God gave man dominion over every living thing that moves upon the earth. She believed that the word "dominion" doesn't imply the right to do as we please with the gifts of Nature. According to her understanding, Adam was meant to be a sort of superintendent of the park—a trustee of the bounties of a plentiful planet.

There are many Old Testament references to support the argument that we humans are not as superior to Nature or as almighty important as we'd like to believe.

Psalm 103:11 says, "As for man, his days are as grass: as a flower of the field so he flourisheth." And Ecclesiastes tells us: "One generation passeth away, and another generation cometh: but the earth abideth forever."

Contrary to what many people may think, the Indians who owned this land before the white man ever put a plow to it, had a highly developed agriculture, and a philosophy about man and his relationship to the land and all living things, including plants.

They believed that the Great Spirit created men to live in harmony with nature and the land. The oldest people in the tribe had the responsibility to see that every child was taught the mysteries of the air, the water, and the land. Every girl and boy was made acquainted with the secrets of growing corn, squash, and beans and how to harvest the wild rice.

The Indians were very successful vegetable gardeners. By the time they introduced the first settlers to corn and squash and beans, they had developed all three vegetables to an amazing degree of sophistication. In the case of corn, or maize, it is almost laughable to compare all the variations and changes our plant scientists have made on it with the improvements and accomplishments of the Indians. The earliest known cultivated ear of corn had only forty-eight kernels. Indian gardeners developed it to yield from five hundred to a thousand kernels an ear. By the time of the first Thanksgiving, they had grown over a thousand varieties, including popcorn, which Squanto served to the Pilgrims as a final delightful touch to that memorable feast.

Other Indian crops included berries (strawberries, gooseberries, raspberries), grapes, plums, persimmons, groundnuts, tuckahoe, rice, cane, prickly pears, nuts (pecans, butternuts, walnuts, hazelnuts, chestnuts, chinquapins), maple sugar, potatoes (sweet and Irish), tobacco, cotton, peanuts, all the edible beans except horsebeans, sunflowers, squashes (hubbard, crooknecked, cymlings, cushaws), field pumpkins, Jerusalem artichokes, tomatoes, garden peppers, pineapples and probably watermelons. (*The Beginnings of Agriculture in America,* Carrier.)

In all, they cultivated, cooked, or ate raw well over 1,000 native plants. With their gifts of corn and potatoes alone, they greatly altered the eating habits and diet of Western civilization.

But to the Indians' way of thinking, working the land and owning it were two opposed concepts. According to them, no one really owns the earth. No matter how much we delude ourselves and each other, the earth belongs to everyone, especially those who come after us—our descendants.

Grandma said they believed that if you want to till the land successfully, you must learn to converse with the spirits that live in the plants, you must be observant in order to see and smell and listen to the weather signs, you must touch the earth to feel if it is ready and willing to be planted. Grandma said there was a whole lot of truth in those Indian beliefs. She taught me that gardening can restore a special sense of harmony with nature in each of us.

For a young boy, growing a garden can be quite an education—at least that was the case when I was planning, planting, weeding, raising, and harvesting vegetables that summer at Grandma Putt's—but in many ways, it was more fun and more satisfying than any classroom experience I have ever had before or since. That season, I learned how to make a plan; how to use my head and back together to make my

32

plan work; that work can be a joy and a pastime, rather than a duty. I learned the extravagant rewards that can result from the practice of simple economies; the usefulness of keeping good and accurate records; the importance of self-reliance. I learned how to observe and converse with nature and the plant people; how to benefit from the good and bad experiences of people far older and wiser than I; what it is to be bone-tired and satisfied at the same time; how to be humble and grateful for a harvest that exceeded my fondest hopes and greatest expectations. And, finally, I learned some of the secrets of good salesmanship.

I wish I could enroll my son Jeff in a course in a school, somewhere, that teaches all those things. But, even though I can't, I know that someday he can learn all of them, and more, in a garden of his own.

Have a Goal When You Begin

Grandma said you should always have a reason to dig into Mother Earth or she won't help you grow anything but weeds. You may never have the need to raise vegetables to feed yourself or your family like so many of the people in other parts of the world. But you would be wise to set yourself or your youngsters a simple, clear-cut purpose for doing it. Otherwise you, or they, may let your minds and muscles wander from the job. Then, the weeds will get the best of your garden, while your vegetables get the worst of it.

Grandma Putt had her own reasons for getting me out into the garden that summer, but she knew they wouldn't carry much weight with me. So, she used the Victory garden idea to get me to look on the project as though it were going to be a great adventure. And that is exactly what it turned out to be.

33

She said she would lend me the money to get started and that I could either pay her back from what I raised and sold, or I could work off what I owed her by weeding and taking care of her garden. She helped me set up some potential customers for my vegetables. These included one of the grocery stores in town and some of the local ladies who did a lot of canning. Grandma said that if I paid her back for her investment, I could use any money left over for war savings stamps. And that if I earned enough to buy a bond, she would match it.

War bonds cost $18.75 and were worth twenty-five bucks. Having that much money, in those days, was tantamount to being rich. The whole idea of doing something for the war effort and filling my wallet at the same time was a goal guaranteed to spark a boy's imagination and kindle his enthusiasm!

That Good Old Garden Plan and What You Need to Know Before You Make It

Funny, how knowing I was eventually going to have to pay back the money I used to start my garden, made even a new gardener like me plan more carefully and plant more wisely.

My entire garden area was only 200 square feet (compare that to the acreage most garden books tell you to plant). My grubstake was just ten dollars.

At first, it was tempting to spend it all at once, to try to get as much planted in that small patch of ground as I possibly could. I quickly realized the folly of my thinking when I took my first plan to Grandma for the money.

She said that a good garden plan can only be drawn up after you get to know your vegetable people, the different types and varieties. She said I would have to learn about their soil requirements, the kind of location they liked to grow in, temperature requirements, and the time it takes them to grow ripe for digging or picking.

In addition to that, she said I'd have to learn a little about "brotherhood gardening," interplanting, succession planting, seeds, seedlings, and the lay of my land. Only then, she said, would I be ready for planting.

How to Know Who's Who in the Vegetable World

It will be helpful to you if you get to know some of the basic things about vegetables before you draw up your planting plans and go buy seeds or seedlings.

Vegetables can be divided into two basic types. Most of them are *annuals* which complete their entire life-cycles in one short growing season. Others, are *perennials* which, if carefully tended, will present you with tasty crops, year after year.

We raise different types of vegetables for their different edible parts—some for their roots, some for their foliage, and some for their fruit or flowers.

It's not always necessary to wait until these plants reach maturity in order to harvest them. In fact, most vegetables are firmest, crispest and tastiest if they are dug up or picked *before* they are full-grown.

For the vegetable gardener, a good general way to tell your vegetable friends apart is by knowing the temperature they prefer to grow in best. Because of their temperature preferences, we often separate vegetables into two crop groups. We call these *cool-season crops* and *warm-season crops*.

COOL-SEASON VEGETABLES
Most of the perennial vegetables grow best in the cool seasons. These include artichokes, asparagus, and rhubarb—or

35

pie plant as my Grandma used to call it. Incidentally, Grandma said, a hard cold rain *will* hurt the rhubarb.

In the very early spring, just as soon as the frost is out of the ground, you can plant: beets, carrots, Chinese mustard, lettuce (several kinds), and onions (either seeds or seedlings).

As soon as all danger of frost has passed, plant: cabbage, broccoli, ·Brussels sprouts, cauliflower, collards, early corn, kale, kohlrabi, leeks, more lettuce, celery, garlic, New Zealand spinach, spinach, early peas, more radishes, salsify, and turnips. This second planting usually can be put in a week or ten days after the first. These plants do have the ability to weather some slight late frosts.

WARM-SEASON VEGETABLES

After all danger of frost is past, you can go ahead and plant your warm-season growers. Included in this group are: green and yellow string (snap) beans, lima beans, borage, chard, Chinese cabbage, cucumbers (early hybrid), endive, muskmelon, more pears (spread them out over several plantings throughout the spring and early summer), peppers, potatoes (white), tomatoes, watermelons and a week or so later, sweet potatoes. Some of these will not begin to grow until after the ground is warmed up to the mid-sixties, but it is all right to put them in a little early.

In July, you will want to plant: more cucumbers, okra, gourds, eggplant, squashes, late cabbage, more beets, more radishes, late corn, late beans, and pumpkins. These will be ready for an autumn harvest.

Growing Times

With the exception of radishes, which will germinate in a few days, few if any vegetables are quick growers. This doesn't stop seedmen from calling anything that takes less than three months to grow a fast-growing variety. You will have to get used to the speed with which Mother Nature and Mother Earth get things done. Once you get into the slow but sure natural swing of things, you will feel more at ease and in tune with your garden.

For a list of approximate growing times, consult your seed packets or the following list and guide.

Vegetable Team Starters

BEANS
60 days

BEETS
Dark Red

BRUSSELS SPROUTS
Long Island Imp. 90 days

F1 HYBRID CABBAGE
Emerald Cross 67 days
Swellhead 95 days
Stone Head 50 days
Jersey Queen 63 days
Golden Acre Resistant 65 days
Marion Market 80 days
Wisconsin All-Season 90 days
Copenhagen Market 67 days
Early Dwarf Flat Dutch 85 days
Late Flat Dutch 100 days
Danish Ballhead 105 days

RED CABBAGE
Mammoth Rock Red 100 days

CAULIFLOWER
Early Snowball "A" 55 days
Snowball "X" 65 days
Snow King 45 days

CELERY
Summer Pascal 110 days

CORN
100 days

CUCUMBER
Ball Early Hybrid 58 days
Hiyield 62 days
Pioneer 55 days
Spartan Valor 60 days
Triple Purpose 54 days
Triumph 60 days

EGGPLANT
Mission Bell 70 days

LETTUCE
Salad Bowl 45 days

MELON
Honey Rock 85 days
Mainerock 75 days
Samson 85–90 days
Saticoy Hybrid 90 days
Super Market 85 days
Watermelon:
Dixie Queen Hybrid 82 days
Sweetmeat 83 days

PEAS
Freezonian 62 days
Canape 62 days
Aconcagua 65 days

Vegetable Team Starters (cont.)

California Wonder Select
72 days
Delaware Belle   75 days
Hungarian Yellow Wax
80 days
Long Red Cayenne   74 days
Mercury   80 days
Merrimack Wonder   68 days
Midway   70 days
Pimento Perfection   75 days
Red Chili   84 days
Sweet Bull Nose   65 days
Titan   75 days
Vinedale   62 days
Yolo Wonder   70 days

RADISH
Cherry Belle   23 days

SPINACH
60 days

SQUASH
Chefini   48 days

TOMATO
Beefsteak   96 days
Bonny Best   70 days
Break O'Day   70 days
Campbell   75 days
Earliana   66 days
Fireball   60 days
Firesteel   68 days
Floradel   82 days
Giant Tree   88 days
Glamour   74 days
Gulf State Market   80 days
Heinz 1350   75 days
Heinz 1370   77 days

Heinz 1439   77 days
Jubilee (TA)   80 days
Manalucie   82 days
Marglobe Supreme (TA)
77 days
New Yorker   62 days
Oxheart   90 days
Ponderosa   95 days
Rome VF   76 days
Rutgers (TA)   82 days
Sunray   83 days
Super Sioux   70 days
Valiant   70 days
Wisconsin Chief   72 days
Gardener's Delight   50 days
Small Fry (TA/JC)   65 days
Tiny Tim (TA)   46 days
Avalanche   77 days
Ball Extra Early (TA)
55 days
Ball Giant Hybrid   65 days
Bonny Best Hybrid   65 days
Bonus   75 days
Burpee Big Boy Hybrid
(TA/JC)   78 days
Burpee Big Early (TA)
62 days
Burpee Hybrid   70 days
Early Salad   45 days
Golden Boy   80 days
Mocross Supreme   70–75 days
Mocross Surprise   60–70 days
Patio (TA)   70 days
Rushmore   66 days
Rutgers Hybrid   85 days
Spring Set VF   65 days
Terrific VFN   73 days
Vineripe   80 days
Wonder Boy (TA)   80 days
Ohio-Indiana   74 days

Brotherhood Gardening

It was from Grandma Putt that I first learned about *companion cropping*, or planting. She called it "brotherhood gardening." She said the idea was very old and is mentioned in the earliest almanacs as "good influence" planting. She said she got the name "brother hood gardening" from a sermon the minister preached right after the 1919 race riots in Chicago. He was a local gardener of some renown, and he told his parishioners they would be wise to take a good hard look at the example of certain dissimilar flowers, herbs, and vegetables which live together in a mutually beneficial way. They help each other by supplying needed nutrients or by warding off insects.

This will give you an idea of how the good-neighbor system works in the world of plants. . . . The Indians taught the colonists to plant corn with pole beans so the cornstalks could help support the beans. Now, we know that the beans also supply needed nitrogen to the corn.

Some good neighbors, like spearmint, tansy, garlic, and onions, can be planted near vegetables or flowers bothered by aphids. They also ward off rabbits who just love your tender young beans and leaf lettuce.

Spearmint and tansy, incidentally, are good for warding off ants. Put some dried spearmint leaves at the back of your pantry shelves if this is a sometimes problem at your house.

Here is a list of recent research on other good plant neighbors. It was compiled by Richard Gregg for the Bio-Dynamic Farming and Gardening Association:

asparagus and tomatoes or asparagus and nasturtiums

beans and carrots, cauliflower, beets, cabbage and cucumbers

beans and potatoes also do very well together; the beans ward off the Colorado potato bugs

wax beans do well with celery if the celery is planted six to one

beets and beans, onions, or kohlrabi

cabbage and potatoes, dill, chamomile, sage, vermouth, rosemary, and the mint family

carrots and lettuce and chives

cauliflower and celery

celery and leeks, tomatoes

corn and potatoes, beans and peas, as well as melons, squash, pumpkins and cucumbers

cucumbers and potatoes, cabbage, radishes

kohlrabi and lettuce; kohlrabi and beets and onions

eggplant and green beans

leeks and celery

lettuce and strawberries, carrots, and radishes

onions and beets

peas and radishes, carrots, cucumbers, corn beans, and turnips

potatoes and beans, cabbage and peas

pumpkins and corn

radishes and peas, lettuce, chervil

spinach and strawberries

tomatoes and asparagus, parsley, cabbage; these also do well with potatoes and cucumbers

THE BASIS FOR OLD-FASHIONED SPRAYS

Four outstanding good-neighbor plants which can help your vegetables are neither herbs nor vegetables; they are flowers. The four I mean are, old-fashioned marigolds (the kind that smell so spicy), nasturtiums, geraniums (both red and white), and poppies. Grandma used all four around the outside border of her vegetable garden. Sometimes she chopped, squeezed, and then mixed them up with an old egg beater to make organic insect repellents. If you try this, be sure to dilute the pulp with ten parts water in your sprayer.

If you live in the south, don't forget to put a few tobacco plants in with your vegetables. They smell wonderful and they are the basis for nicotinia, one of the very best bug killers you can buy.

TRAP PLANTS: THE SACRIFICIAL LAMBS

There may be times when it seems as though your garden is going buggy . . . and to the rabbits, moles, etc. Don't give up! Organic gardeners and old gardening hands who shy away from chemical insecticides have come up with *trap planting*. These plants lure away the insects and animal enemies from nearby vegetables. They are sort of sacrificial lambs which leave themselves wide open to attack in order that your favorite vegetables may survive. Grandma used dill to trap tomato worms, and zinnias and knotweed to attract Japanese beetles.

THE "BAD NEIGHBORS" AND "ARCHIE BUNKER"

Just like people, some plants just can't seem to get along with certain others. It's not that they're mean or misguided, it's just that they both need the same nutrients from the soil or attract the same kinds of insect enemies. One plant, the white potato is a real "Archie Bunker." It doesn't get along with anyone else in the vegetable patch. Here is a list of some vegetables who make bad neighbors. Try not to plant them too close together or they will hurt each others' chances of being healthy and productive.

Mr. Potato is a loner and a bigot, he just doesn't like anyone to move into his neighborhood, especially pumpkins, sunflowers, tomatoes, or raspberries.

Asparagus doesn't get along very well with onions, leeks, garlic, and glads; neither does Benny the bean.

Pole beans also have onion problems and so do bush beans (maybe it's their breath). Pole beans also have their troubles with sunflowers, kohlrabi, and beets.

Beets feel the same way about pole beans, so keep them at opposite sides of the tracks.

Most members of the cabbage family can't stand strawberries, dislike tomatoes and would just rather not live with pole beans.

Carrots don't dig dill.

Chives and peas are not on speaking terms.

Cucumbers are not fans of potatoes or any of the folk from the herb family.

Peas share some of the legume family's prejudices against the onion and garlic guys.

Pumpkins don't like potatoes in their neck of the woods, and strawberries think certain members of the cabbage family stink.

Corn and celery like everybody.

If you match these natural prejudices against the good-neighbor list, you'll be able to plant a garden that will make everyone comfortable.

Interplanting

Some of the "good neighbors" can help save space in your garden. For instance, you can plant radishes between cucumbers and squash. And, of course, pumpkins between rows of corn. This space-saving system is sometimes called *interplanting*. You can also use interplanting to properly use space by planting fast-growing varieties in the same rows as slow growers.

Succession Planting

Never having gardened before, I thought I would have to do my vegetable planting all at once, and that then it would be over for the whole year. Grandma explained that a smart gardener uses *succession planting*. That is, he keeps taking out the spent crops and putting in new ones. He does this all during the spring and summer. Early corn, early peas, lettuce, carrots, radishes, broccoli, and turnips will finish maturing in plenty of time for successive plantings of other crops.

It's even possible to plant in the early fall, before the first frost. At that time, put in: celery, kale, garlic, turnips, or artichokes, rhubarb and asparagus cuttings. However, Grandma preferred to plant the perennials in the very early spring.

Another method of succession planting that guarantees a steady supply of your favorite vegetable crops, is to plant them several times in a series all during the spring and on into early summer. Make your plantings ten days to two weeks apart.

Here is a list of good plant "leaders" and their "followers" to use in your succession planting:

Early peas, followed by early corn, then late snap beans.
Late peas are replaced by corn and then by radishes and
lettuce with spinach.
Onion sets are followed by tomatoes.
Cabbage is the starter and is replaced by lima beans.
Spinach is followed by wax beans.
White radishes start and snap beans finish.

Most seed packets tell you whether the enclosed variety is
for early, midseason, or late planting. By using this information and paying careful attention to the good-neighbor and
bad-neighbor lists, you will be able to keep changing your
garden, and make it a comfortable place for your plants to
live all through the growing season.

Selection

Now just a few words about selection before you complete
your plan and begin planting your garden.

If you are just a beginning gardener and aren't certain how
much work you want to put into it—I suggest the following
varieties and quantities of seeds.

1 packet long green cucumbers
1 packet Chantenay carrots
1 packet Nantes Coreless carrots
1 packet Detroit Dark Red beets
1 packet Black-seeded Simpson lettuce
1 packet Hollow Crown parsnips
1 packet New Crimson Giant radishes
1 packet White Icicle radishes

1 packet Nabel's Giant thick-leaf spinach
1 packet Rutgers tomatoes
1 packet Golden Cross Bantam Sweet corn
1 packet Little Marvel peas
1 packet Burpee's Stringless green bush bean
1 pound yellow onion sets
1 pound white onion sets

If you plant this selection on a ten-by-ten-foot patch in full sun with good drainage, you will be able to supply your family (six people) with fresh vegetables from early summer to the first heavy frost.

Now, for an added treat, why don't you try planting strawberries on three sides of your garden. Use twenty-five plants of Fairfax (they'll come up early), twenty-five plants of Sure Crop Midseason, and twenty-five plants of Sparkle, the late berry.

If you'd like to try raspberries, look for a slightly damp spot in the garden. There you can plant ten raspberries in a four-foot square between your other plants. I suggest Sentry red. It's a new variety developed and tested as being one of the best for the home gardener. Bluecrop or Berkeley blueberries will do just as nicely in that same spot. Make sure varieties you select grow well in your locale. Agricultural Extension Services can recommend those best suited for your use. Take maintenance time, harvest time, and preservability into consideration.

Be sure to include in your garden, vegetables that *you* like. This is especially important if *you* are going to be doing all the gardening work. Then poll everyone in the family for individual favorites. Add as many of these as you can.

Every year, you should try to include at least one vegetable that is new to you and your family. Don't let a neighbor or your own bad experience with canned or frozen samples of a vegetable steer you off it. Somehow, each one improves when it's fresh-picked out of your garden and cooked immediately.

Here is a list of forgotten or ignored vegetables that may become exciting discoveries for you and yours this season. At one time or another, most of these appeared in Grandma Putt's garden. Some of them are old standbys that have dropped out of common use. Others may not be very easy to find. So, study your seed catalogs and scout your nursery carefully to see what you can come up with.

Forgotten and Ignored Vegetables

Leafy Vegetables
borage
burnet
corn salad
Chinese cabbage
  (bak choy)
Chinese mustard
collard
cress
dandelion
day lily
good King Henry
kale
kohlrabi
mustard greens
lovage
orache
rampion
roquette

sea kale
watercress
wood sorrel

Root Crops
celeriac
chicory (also leaves)
black salsify
  (viper's grass)
caraway (also seeds)
golden thistle
  (Spanish oyster plant)
groundnuts (Indian potatoes)
hamburg rooted parsley
Indian breadroot
rocambole
salsify (oyster plant)
skirret
solanum commersoni

turnip-rooted chervil
tuckahoe
wapato
Jerusalem artichokes

Stalks and Shoots
bean sprouts
alexander
angelica
cardoon
samphire

sweet Cicely (also roots)
udo

Seed Pods
black-eyed peas
lentil
Martynia
pea pods
peanuts
okra
Chinese okra

Some of these may be grown commonly in your area of the country, if so, that's all the more reason to include them as possibilities for your garden. If they are strange to you, check them out to see if they will thrive in your area. It never hurts to experiment.

SEED PACKETS

Try to buy fresh seed when you can get it. Sometimes dime-store and grocery-store seed is old. Usually it says on the packet where the seed came from and how old it is. Lots of people swear that garden seeds stored for more than a year are worthless. This just is not so. The longevity of seeds depends on where you got it and how it was stored. Keeping seeds in stoppered bottles in a cool place like a basement will give them at least two years of life, and probably several more. You can usually depend on seed from the old reliable firms. If you are in doubt, you might try starting your seeds indoors for later transplanting outside.

SEEDLINGS

You may want to purchase some plants as partly grown seedlings, ready for transplanting into your garden. Most nurseries have a limited selection of seedlings for the home gardener, but you will almost certainly be able to find tomatoes. More than likely, cabbage, peppers, and chives will be available.

Buying seedlings is more expensive than growing your own plants from seed, but there are some advantages. One is that your plants will have a good healthy start before they go into your garden. Seedlings are especially economical when you only want a few plants. By using them, you'll be getting the jump on Mother Earth's timetable. And, by thoughtful planting, you'll eliminate the crucial *thinning* step for some of your vegetables.

A compromise between buying seeds and buying seedlings is to grow your own seedlings with purchased seeds. You can do this indoors where it can be fun and an educational project for the entire family.

The Lay of the Land

If, as I suggested in the last chapter, you deep-ploughed or spaded your garden patch in the fall and then worked the topsoil with a roto-tiller or a hoe and rake in the spring, you are probably all ready to plant. Oldtimers say the garden surface should have a slight crown at the top and taper off on all four sides. That way, an excess of water from heavy spring showers or summer thunderstorms will run off.

If you don't have much planting space, you'll want to make the most of every bit you do have. Most folks will tell you that the best growing gardens face east or south with the rows laid out from north to south. That's all right unless you happen to be gardening on a slope. Then you will either have to terrace your rows, or, at least, run them across it rather than up and down the hill.

When you draw up your plan, be careful not to allow tall growing plants to block out the sun of those which grow close to the ground. Place corn to the north of your bed, also pole beans, wired peas, staked tomatoes and so on. Low plants, like root crops and leafy vegetables should be to the south. Lettuce and some of the leafy vegetables can stand some shade but potatoes and tomatoes require lots of sun.

Some plants are real space stealers. Perhaps the first among these is potatoes. If you don't have a very big planting bed, my advice is to forget them. They are susceptible to disease and, since they store well, are almost always available at your nearest produce counter. If you do have the room, plant 'em. Just like all your vegetable friends, they taste best when they're home grown.

Revamping an Older Garden

If yours is not a new garden but one that you've been working for several years, perhaps this is the year you should revamp some of your usual thinking.

For too many years, most of us have planted traditional and stereotyped vegetable gardens. They all look the same, like a miniature field of farm crops: Rows of radishes, rows of corn, carrots, and lettuce, we make sure that we keep each separated from the other and in a straight line. Then to compound the felony, we plant the same thing in the same part of the garden year after year.

Now we wonder why the production gets lower and lower every year. The answer is simple. Each plant extracts certain elements from the soil to help carry out needed chemical processes within its system. After a couple of years in the same spot it will take all those needed elements from the soil. "The soil is like a table full of food, each plant that sits down at it, makes it less."

Rotate Your Crops

The answer is as old as the Indians and as sure as the Bible—*crop rotation*. Keep your vegetable plantings moving from year to year. Never let crops be planted in the same place that they were last season or the previous planting if you are using succession planting methods.

Give That Old Garden Soil a Booster Shot

Each new season, you should give your garden soil a dose of fertilizer to prepare it for those rough weeks ahead, much in the same way that we give our kids a booster shot before flu season comes. You can do this by mixing up a batch of old-fashioned "barnyard tea."

Barnyard Tea

To make barnyard tea, mix together fifty pounds of manure, fifty pounds of peat moss, twenty-five to fifty pounds of garden gypsum, and twenty-five pounds of garden food. Apply this, along with liberal quantities of leaves, over each 100 to 150 square feet of garden area in the fall, winter, or the very early spring.

In most areas of the north, barnyard tea should be spaded into the soil in late April or early May before you plant your new crops.

I want to remind you that the timing for these applications depends entirely on your local climate and soil temperature conditions. If your garden is located in a valley, it will take several more weeks to be ready for growing than if it is located on higher ground where the dampness and moisture can be baked out more quickly by the sun.

This procedure returns more of the elements to the soil than your plants extracted from it last season.

Grandma's Garden Diary

You'll notice that I've already mentioned drawing up a planting plan for your garden half a dozen times. That's because planning is one of the two or three most important steps in vegetable gardening.

When you've made your final selections for the first planting, go ahead and put that crop in the ground. Then record the date, the location, and the expected growing time for each vegetable you plant. You can get these expected growing times from the list I included earlier, from seed catalogs, or on the backs of your seed packets.

Of course, it will be a miracle if any plant comes up exactly on the numbered day these reference guides say they will. Your plantings will germinate and grow according to local soil conditions, temperature, climate, and moisture. The references listing the number of days of growing time relate to ideal situations set up by the seedsmen to study their new offerings and old standbys. Give yourself ample leeway on

HARD-FROST DATES
From U.S.D.A. weather records

State	First in Fall	Last in Spring
Alabama, N. W.	Oct. 30	Mar. 25
Alabama, S. E.	Nov. 15	Mar. 8
Arizona, No.	Oct. 19	Apr. 23
Arizona, So.	Dec. 1	Mar. 1
Arkansas, No.	Oct. 23	Apr. 7
Arkansas, So.	Nov. 3	Mar. 25
California		
Imperial Valley	Dec. 15	Jan. 25
Interior Valley	Nov. 15	Mar. 1
Southern Coast	Dec. 15	Jan. 15
Central Coast	Dec. 1	Feb. 25
Mountain Sections	Sept. 1	Apr. 25
Colorado, West	Sept. 18	May 25
Colorado, N. E.	Sept. 27	May 11
Colorado, S. E.	Oct. 15	May 1
Connecticut	Oct. 20	Apr. 25
Delaware	Oct. 25	Apr. 15
District of Columbia	Oct. 23	Apr. 11
Florida, No.	Dec. 5	Feb. 25
Florida, Cen.	Dec. 28	Feb. 11
Florida, South of Lake Okeechobee, almost frost-free		
Georgia, No.	Nov. 1	Apr. 1
Georgia, So.	Nov. 15	Mar. 15
Idaho	Sept. 22	May 21
Illinois, No.	Oct. 8	May 1
Illinois, So.	Oct. 20	Apr. 15
Indiana, No.	Oct. 8	May 1
Indiana, So.	Oct. 20	Apr. 15
Iowa, No.	Oct. 2	May 1
Iowa, So.	Oct. 9	Apr. 15
Kansas	Oct. 15	Apr. 20
Kentucky	Oct. 20	Apr. 15
Louisiana, No.	Nov. 10	Mar. 13
Louisiana, So.	Nov. 20	Feb. 20
Maine	Sept. 25	May 25
Maryland	Oct. 20	Apr. 19
Massachusetts	Oct. 25	Apr. 25
Michigan, Upper Pen.	Sept. 15	May 25
Michigan, No.	Sept. 25	May 17
Michigan, So.	Oct. 8	May 10
Minnesota, No.	Sept. 15	May 25
Minnesota, So.	Oct. 1	May 11
Mississippi, No.	Oct. 30	Mar. 25
Mississippi, So.	Nov. 15	Mar. 15
Missouri	Oct. 20	Apr. 20
Montana	Sept. 22	May 21
Nebraska, W.	Oct. 4	May 11
Nebraska, E.	Oct. 15	Apr. 15
Nevada, W.	Sept. 22	May 19
Nevada, E.	Sept. 14	June 1
New Hampshire	Sept. 25	May 23
New Jersey	Oct. 25	Apr. 20
New Mexico, No.	Oct. 17	Apr. 23
New Mexico, So.	Nov. 1	Apr. 1
New York, W.	Oct. 8	May 10
New York, E.	Oct. 15	May 1
New York, No.	Oct. 1	May 15
N. Carolina, W.	Oct. 25	Apr. 15
N. Carolina, E.	Nov. 1	Apr. 8
N. Dakota	Sept. 13	May 21
N. Dakota, E.	Sept. 20	May 16
Ohio, No.	Oct. 15	May 6
Ohio, So.	Oct. 20	Apr. 20
Oklahoma	Nov. 2	Apr. 2
Oregon, W.	Oct. 25	Apr. 17
Oregon, E.	Sept. 22	June 4
Pennsylvania, W.	Oct. ·10	Apr. 20
Pennsylvania, Cen.	Oct. 15	May 1
Pennsylvania, E.	Oct. 15	Apr. 17
Rhode Island	Oct. 25	Apr. 25
S. Carolina, N. W.	Nov. 8	Apr. 1
S. Carolina, S. E.	Nov. 15	Mar. 15
S. Dakota	Sept. 25	May 15
Tennessee	Oct. 25	Apr. 10
Texas, N. W.	Nov. 1	Apr. 15
Texas, N. E.	Nov. 10	Mar. 21
Texas, So.	Dec. 15	Feb. 10
Utah	Oct. 19	Apr. 26
Vermont	Sept. 25	May 23
Virginia, No.	Oct. 25	Apr. 15
Virginia, So.	Oct. 30	Apr. 10
Washington, W.	Nov. 15	Apr. 10
Washington, E.	Oct. 1	May 15
W. Virginia, W.	Oct. 15	May 1
W. Virginia, E.	Oct. 1	May 15
Wisconsin, No.	Sept. 25	May 17
Wisconsin, So.	Oct. 10	May 1
Wyoming, W.	Aug. 20	June 20
Wyoming, E.	Sept. 20	May 21

either side of the expected growing time. You can judge this leeway based on your local weather.

Having a record of each planting according to the variety, expected growing time, location, and success or failure of the crop, is as important as having a plan. You should keep these records up all through the season and from year to year. They will help you remember how each variety thrived under your local conditions; if it took a longer or shorter time to grow, and whether the vegetable you harvested turned out to be tasty or bad. Using these records, you will be better prepared to decide what to plant next year.

Another reason to keep records as to placement of each vegetable is so you will remember *not* to plant the same type of plant in the same spot next season. Continued plantings in the same location take too many of the same nutrients from the soil and make the next planting much more susceptible to disease.

After several years of *accurate record-keeping,* you will have a good idea of which plants do best in your garden and when they should be planted. This is valuable information you'll never get from any general source material, so start keeping records during your first year of gardening and keep up the good work.

Grandma Putt kept a yearly garden notebook, so filled with detailed information and observations that I wish I had one now to aid me in writing this book.

Tools of the Gardener's Trade

Whenever I complained that I needed this or that tool to get a particular gardening job accomplished, Grandma laughed and said that most of the Indian tribes got by with a moose-antler rake, a clam-shell hoe and a deer-horn planting stick.

Garden Notebook

April 18

Lots of mixed sun and showers this month. Unusually warm all this week. Ground should be warm enough soon for successful early planting.

April 28

Had Junior spade up vegetable patch. Soil moist and crumbly. Will begin planting tomorrow. Moving corn and beans to N.W. corner this year - opposite last year's.

April 29

Hill-planted corn and beans. Used Tender Crop stringless beans again - two packets. Tried one packet Marcross early corn along with my usual Golden Cross Bantam. Sarah Amos says its the sweetest early variety. We'll see. Put in four rows carrots (one more than last year.) Rows fifteen inches apart - one inch deep. Chantenay red core type — These did well last year. Junior raked in root crop maggot control before planting carrots, radishes and beets. Maybe the cutworms will leave us alone this year.

June 2

Beets are nearly ready for thinning now.

To be perfectly honest, you can plant and grow a beautiful garden with three or four basic tools. They are: a spade, a rake, a hoe, and a small hand trowel. Don't even begin to begin without the first three.

But if you are like me and most other gardeners, it won't be long before you begin to accumulate a number of other useful, if less important, items. They are:

1. a broad-tined vegetable fork for digging;
2. plenty of garden hose, a bucket, a watering can, and a plastic or canvas soaking hose;
3. a compression sprayer, for controlled and precise weed-killing;
4. a Warren hoe, that's v-shaped for easy furrowing;
5. several sizes of wooden baskets for harvesting.

If you really take to gardening in a big way, you may want to purchase a mulcher, or a mulching attachment for your power lawn mower, and, last—and most expensive—a roto-tiller. If the prices of roto-tillers turns you off, you can use an old-fashioned hand-pushed cultivator. It will do the job just as well with a little more effort on your part.

A list of garden tools can become practically endless. If you are one of those bright-eyed American tool-collectors who turn up in all the garden centers and hardware stores every spring, it will pay to buy a wheelbarrow.

Now, Take a Deep Breath . . . And Get Planting!

After I had followed all the steps necessary to get my soil ready for planting that are described in this and the last chapter, Grandma had me give my garden patch a good and thorough soaking.

For planting, the soil should be moist clear through, but not cold and muddy. Pick up a handful. It should be moist enough to pack, and still dry enough to crumble easily through your fingers.

Grandma said, "Plant in the morning, harvest in the evening." This is another old saying that bears up under close scientific study and experimentation. Remember, plants are like people. It's expecting a lot to ask them to begin work during the hottest part of the day. When planting, remember, only "mad dogs and Englishmen go out in the noonday sun!"

There are several methods of planting a garden. All of them are as old and time-proven as the Ten Commandments. You can choose whichever way suits the lay of your land and appeals to your sense of order and aesthetics. I include in these methods: surface planting, raised-bed planting, single- and double-row planting, hill planting, mound planting, contouring, terracing, and irrigating.

Surface Planting

Most gardens all over the world are planted at the surface level of the field or patch as it is in nature. This method inhibits the tendency of the soil to dry out from the sun. You can water with a soaking hose or a sprinkler. But remember most vegetables don't like to have their leaves wet all the time. Deep watering is best.

Raised-Bed Planting

This is the old-fashioned method of planting used in the Low Countries of northern Europe where heavy rainfall is a normal weather condition in the spring and early summer.

Use your spade or hoe to dig foot-deep furrows between rows. These furrows should be sloped on a downward grade to meet a drainage trench at the low end of the rows.

Pile excess soil on either side of the furrows and work in compost and garden gypsum for a fine seed bed.

Soak the furrows thoroughly with an open end hose or a soaking hose. If you live where there are dry soil conditions, don't use this system as the soil in the raised beds may dry out too quickly.

Single- And Double-Row Planting

Single-row planting is a compromise between surface and raised-bed planting. The furrows are hoed to a depth of only four to six inches, and the seed is planted toward the southern edge of the furrow bank.

Double-row planting is just what the term implies. You put in two rows of vegetables like carrots, radishes, turnips, or onions in parallel rows about two feet apart.

In between the double rows, dig a slight depression for easy watering with a soaking hose.

Hill Planting

After you read this you will know what people mean when they say they don't give a hill of beans. Beans and corn have been planted in hills since Indian times. The only trouble with the term is that the "hills" are not hills, but circles.

The Indians planted about a half dozen kernels of corn in a two-foot circle around a dead fish. Even in pre-Columbian times, they were apparently aware of the beneficial and fertilizing qualities of decaying animal matter.

This method of planting will give you lots of room for interplanting beans, squash and pumpkins. These are the other members of the North American Indians big four vegetable crops.

You will have to quickly thin your seedlings to the healthiest two or three as soon as they have developed two leaves. Proper thinning will help you have a good harvest, so don't be timid about it.

Mound Planting

Another Indian method of planting, similar to hill planting, is mound planting. Place corn, muskmelons, and watermelons in little mounds of soil about a square foot or more. Thin them out when they're up. Furrow around the mounds, and keep well irrigated.

Contour Planting and Terracing

The Babylonians, the Incas, and the Tibetans are just three ancient peoples who used contour planting and terracing methods to grow their crops on slopes and mountainsides. You may need to use these systems if your garden area has a deep grade to it.

If the grade is gentle, plant across the slope following the contour of your land.

If the slope is steep, you will probably have to make several flattened terraces or steps across the slope to accommodate your plants. These can be several rows deep.

Like the Incans, you will find that it's easier to water these crops from above by digging simple irrigation trenches and a series of board dams to hold the water at each terrace long enough to soak the ground thoroughly.

Irrigation

If you live in the hot southwest, or where drought is a problem, you may have to irrigate your garden by digging the furrows deep enough to carry a flow of ground water. This will be especially important where there are light sandy soils which do not hold the moisture very long. Write your local Agriculture Extension Office for free bulletins which outline simple and practical methods of irrigating.

Planting Tips

Take some wooden pegs or stakes soaked in linseed oil and mark off your boundaries and rows for each variety of vegetable you intend to plant. Then, select your planting method and go to it.

Around the outside border of your garden, plant red and white geraniums on one side, nasturtiums on another, poppies on a third, and old-fashioned marigolds on the fourth. Also, mix these plants among the vegetables taking care to consult the bad-neighbor list quoted earlier. If you live in the south, intermix some tobacco plants in the border and among the vegetables.

Remember that it's not necessary to segregate each plant to its own kind. Use the techniques of brotherhood gardening, interplanting fast and slow-growers and crop rotation.

The rows you lay out should run east and west to insure that each of your plant friends gets his fair share of sun.

These rows should be no longer than ten feet if you're a beginner at the gardening game. And they don't have to cross the whole width of your vegetable patch. Leave a path, or several paths through your garden depending on its size. Plant taller growing plants at the high end of your patch so they won't block the sun from the lower growing varieties.

Vegetable gardens have been too stereotyped-looking too long. Use your ingenuity and knowledge of different planting methods to create some interesting patterns.

Watering

I've already tried to make all the important points in regard to watering your vegetable garden.

When the seeds are planted and the seedlings are first up, it's important to keep the top two or three inches of surface soil consistently moist.

After they begin to grow, most vegetables should be watered regularly and not allowed to dry out. But don't overwater during hot spells. This will weaken your plants at the roots and make them susceptible to root rot and other fungus diseases.

Most vegetables would rather have their roots watered than their tops. This is especially true of Timothy tomato and Mercedes melon. This does not mean they don't appreciate you giving their foliage a shower from time to time.

Singing in the Shower

To give your vegetables a shower, dilute one part of biodegradable dishwashing soap (my Grandma used Fels-Naphtha) in ten parts of water. Spray this solution on your plants' foliage in a fine mist. Use a high compression tank-type sprayer, a plunger-type sprayer, or a hose-end sprayer to do the job. Treat your plant people to these showers two or three times each season. Showers will discourage insect pests who dislike the taste of soap, and they will act as a surface-active agent on the leaf surfaces, improving respiration and increasing the plants ability to carry on photosyntheses.

Feeding

If you feed your plants well and often, you will eat well and often after you harvest them. Grandma recommended the "little bit lots of times" method, as opposed to "lots of food one time."

Set your spreader on its lowest setting. Use a 5-20-20 dry fertilizer; also bone meal or any of the fish emulsions whenever you get the ambition.

Stir, Stir, Stir Your Soil

"Stir the soil!" That was the catch-phrase of the old-time vegetable gardeners. Use a hoe or cultivator . . . and, if you can, a reliable small boy. Be careful not to disturb the roots of your plants. If you hoe thoroughly two or three times after planting, you and your plants won't have much trouble with weeds all summer.

Using your hoe, rake, and cultivator will create a good layer of surface mulch, allow your plants' roots to breathe and keep weeds to a minimum. And the well-cultivated, loose, friable surface soil will hold more moisture during dry spells.

Mulching

Keep your vegetables cool and moist by mulching their feet with wood chips and old newspapers that have been soaked in liquid manure. Liquid manure is made by soaking a bag or gunny sack of dry manure in water. Be careful not to get this liquid on the leaves or foliage of young plants. Using a mulch of old newspapers wasn't very patriotic during WW II, but, these days, it's a recommended practice of those who advocate good ecology. The wood-pulp in newsprint is organic and will eventually biodegrade and return to the soil.

PLANTING THROUGH YOUR NEWSPAPER MULCH

You can plant through these newspaper mulches. Stretch the newspaper out from one end of the row to another and anchor it to the soil with rocks or wooden pegs. Next, cut holes through the newspaper to plant through. As the plants grow, they'll be protected from weeds and many pests. The newspapers will keep the soil surface moist, warm, and weed-free. Then as the days get hotter, they'll ward off the scorching sun, insects and fungus diseases.

OTHER GOOD MULCHES

If you happen to take after the Collier brothers and have other good uses for your old newspapers, here are some recommended mulches you can use.

> leaf mold
> lignified wood
> pine needles
> sawdust
> clean straw
> redwood shavings
> processed manure

62

black plastic sheeting
fallen leaves

Be sure to make your mulches two or more inches thick. If you do, you won't be troubled by weeds.

Getting the Bugs Out and Fighting Off Disease

As far as my Grandma and I are concerned, the best program for fighting off bugs and disease in your garden is a preventive program. By that I mean, use the time-tested good cultural practices. Make sure your plants get plenty of sunlight. Water, feed, and weed them regularly. Stir up the soil. Use effective mulches. And, give them a shower with soap and water from time to time. Chances are that the healthy plants that result from these practices will be able to fight off most bugs and shake off any disease without any additional help from you. These garden enemies are born bullies and almost always pick on plants that are weaklings.

When you begin to garden and grow vegetables, you will be bombarded with literature containing claims and counterclaims by those in favor or opposed to the use of chemical controls for insects and diseases.

I favor Grandma Putt's commonsense methods. She practiced insect, weed, and disease control in a manner that let "the punishment fit the crime." She never needlessly used a strong chemical unless it became absolutely necessary . . . and only after all other methods failed.

BE DIPLOMATIC, GET SOME ALLIES TO FIGHT WITH YOU

Grandma approved of attracting birds to the garden to fight alongside her in the war against bugs. She said a couple of robins are worth all the berries and cherries they will eat.

Robins prefer a meat diet and that means, look out bugs, grubs, and worms! Put some bird houses and feeding stations around your garden area. Especially try to attract members of the finch family. They eat lots of weed seed. Don't overfeed your allies with bird seed. Leave some room in their stomachs for a few bugs.

She approved of my catching toads, to put under some shady plant, and ladybugs for the tomatoes. Nor was she the slightest bit squeamish about encouraging me to bring home a garter snake or two. She even had me place a pile of sticks near the corn where these bug-eating snakes could live. These allies are the predators of the bug world and will do much to control insect pests even in years when they are a real nuisance.

Don't be above picking bugs and caterpillars or moths off your plants. Believe me, this may be old-fashioned, but it works. Just drop them in a jar of kerosene. As soon as you see your first enemy, sneak up and pick him off—before long you'll be a pro.

DON'T FEEL GUILTY ABOUT USING CHEMICALS

My grandmother Puttnam was the best and most successful gardener I've ever known. She never hesitated to use sprays in her garden, or dust, or any other preparation that would get rid of her garden enemies. She was more in touch with nature and the natural way of things than anyone I've ever met. But she knew that chemicals could be used wisely and carefully to help man harness nature on farms and in gardens. She said that Nature can lose control once in a while, just like men, and that the Bible is full of plenty of examples of locusts, plagues, and pestilence. Sure, we have made some mistakes and overused some chemicals that have left harmful residues, but they have been relegated to the waste dump. No one in his right mind would suggest that we get rid of penicillin, Aureomycin, or polio vaccine. The important thing to repeat to yourself is . . . use chemicals for the right job, wisely and carefully. Please follow the directions on the package.

My Baker's Dozen Spraying Commandments

1. Select the right sprayer for the job. Buy the best quality you can afford. It will make spraying easier and, with good care, your sprayer will last for years. And be sure to get one that gives you full control of spray mix and application!

2. Before you spray, be sure to read *all* the sprayer directions—right down to the warranty. "Test drive" your new sprayer using water to see how it works and what it will do.

3. Mix your spray materials *exactly* according to instructions.

4. Choose the right pressure. Use high pressure for a fine, penetrating mist (good for flowers). Use lower pressure if you want a heavier, wetting, nondrift spray (best for weeds).

5. *Spot spray,* don't broadcast. Spray only to the point of run-off. Avoid drenching. And waste.

6. Spray where the trouble is. Because most trouble starts *under* the plant leaves, it is especially important that you spray there. Cover the entire stem system too. Spraying on target avoids waste in time and material.

7. Use an adjustable nozzle to produce a fine cone-shaped mist for closeup applications and a coarser spray for long-range spraying or for weeds.

8. For maximum effectiveness—not to mention less wear and tear on you—spray in the cool of the day.

9. To prevent drifting of spray to nontarget areas, don't spray when the wind is blowing.

10. If you prefer to dust plants, apply the dust in the morning or evening when the air is still and when dew on the plants makes the dust stick better.

11. Dress sensibly. Don't wear shorts or a bathing suit. It's a good idea to wear gloves (plastic throw-aways will do) and a hat if you're spraying above your head or at eye level. Wear shoes.

12. Thoroughly drain and clean your sprayer when finished. Use a mild solution of warm soap and water. Wipe your equipment dry when finished. Good care will make it last many, many seasons.

13. Store sprays and dusts out of reach of children, preferably in a locked cabinet. Keep sprays in original containers. Be sure labels are kept on containers. Do not burn empty containers.

My Handy List of Government-Approved Plant Medications

The U.S. Environmental Protection Agency or your local State Department of Agriculture today approves all spray materials sold in garden centers and hardware stores. Most sprays are relatively short-lived: all are safe for use in the home garden when used as directed. If you have questions regarding use and application in your area, consult your store, university extension service, or a garden club.

The following is a list of common yard and garden problems and the spray materials often recommended by gardening experts to control to control them. Many of these insecticides and fungicides are mixed and available in standard formulations to give more general control of pests.

PEST	WHAT TO USE	SUGGESTIONS
ants	chlordane, Diazinon	Apply when present. Try to locate and treat their nests.
aphids	Diazinon, Malathion, nicotine sulphate pyrethrum, rotenone	Spray foliage thoroughly with force. Repeat as needed.
beetles	Carbaryl (Sevin), Diazinon, Malathion	Recommend wettable powder formulations on fruits and vegetables.
borers	Carbaryl, lindane	Care and timing important to kill eggs in egg-laying period.
caterpillars	Carbaryl, Diazinon, Malathion, oil spray, rotenone	Short residual life. Use oil spray in water in very early spring for over-wintering eggs.
chinch bugs and sod webworms	Aspon, Carbaryl, Diazinon, Malathion, Trithion	Spray lawns when bugs first become present. Water well into thatch. Spray lawn edges thoroughly.
cutworms	Carbaryl, Diazinon	Do not spray Diazinon on foliage.
grasshoppers	Carbaryl, Diazinon Malathion	Spray foliage when grass-hoppers are present.
gypsy moths	Carbaryl, meth-oxychlor	Carbaryl has residual life for about five days. Spray tree crowns well.
Japanese beetles	Carbaryl, Malathion	Apply as necessary.
leafhoppers	Diazinon, Malathion, Meta Systox-R	Spray foliage thoroughly when mines appear. Repeat in 10-12 days.

mites (red spiders)	Diazinon, Dicofol (Kelthane), Malathion, oil spray	Be sure to treat underside of leaves. Apply 2-3 times at weekly intervals. Apply oil spray in early spring.
fleas, ticks	Carbaryl, Diazinon	Spray cracks and crevices.
mosquitoes	Malathion, pyrethrum	Also eliminate all standing water that mosquitoes use as breeding grounds. Spray underneath leaves, foundations, under porches where mosquitoes rest.
snails, slugs	metaldehyde	Spray infested areas especially near borders and lawn edges. Control is slow but sure.
scale insects	Carbaryl, Diazinon, Malathion, oil spray	Spray in "crawler" stage, usually late spring; certain soft-scale species hatch in late summer, early fall. Apply dormant sprays before new growth appears; repeat spraying may be necessary.
tarnished plant bugs	Carbaryl, Diazinon, Malathion	Best control achieved when bugs are small (nymph stage).
tent caterpillar	Carbaryl, Diazinon, Malathion	Spray when nests are first noticed. Care must be taken to spray tree thoroughly.
termites	chlordane	For best control, long residual life is required in soil and under buildings.
thrips	Carbaryl, Diazinon, Malathion, rotenone	Tiny insects; often feed inside buds and scar foliage. Weekly spraying may be needed.
worms (bag, web and canker)	Carbaryl, Diazinon, dormant oils, Malathion	Apply oil spray for dormant eggs. Bagworms best controlled in early summer.

black spot	Benlate, Maneb (Fore or Dithane M-22 Special or Dithane M-45), Folpet	Thorough coverage of all plant surfaces necessary.
chickweed, knot-weed, clover	Dicamba, MCPP, 2,4,5-TP (Silvex)	Repeated applications may be necessary. Be careful on sensitive southern grasses.
crabgrass	ammonium methyl arsenate	For post-emergence. Use with care. Even application important.
dandelions,	2,4-D	Care needed when using volatile esters. Use one-half rate on some southern grasses.
powdery mildew	Acti-Dione PM, Dinocap (Karathane)	Thorough coverage of all plant surfaces necessary.

Put a Lightning Rod Over Your Garden and Watch It Grow!

A thunder-and-lightning storm has an extremely fertilizing effect ·on your garden and lawn. Immediately after one of these supercharged storms your plants seem, literally, to turn green on the spot. Fact of the matter is, my friends, they do, as a result of electrically charging the oxygen which turns into 78 percent nitrogen.

You can create this same condition in your garden by practicing a special type of gardening called *electroculture*. Electroculture is gardening with the use of metal objects, such as copper wire, metal trellises, and tin cans to attract static electricity to the soil and the immediate atmosphere of your vegetable garden. This charges your garden, and the flow of elements will increase the size, health, and yield of your crops.

Grandma said that when Great-Grandpa Coolidge was a young man, electroculture was all the rage in the agricultural journals and periodicals of the day. This growing method was first discovered and practiced in Europe, but when it was brought to our shores it spread like wildfire among the faddist farmers. Then, like many good things that are over-praised and overpublicized, electroculture fell into disrepute. I believe that if you approach it gingerly, and use it sparingly, you will have some very good results raising vegetables with electroculture.

HOW-TO-DO-IT ELECTROCULTURE TIPS

Here's how to grow vegetables with electroculture. First, stretch a piece of fine copper wire over the top of your vegetables, and fasten it to wooden stakes at each end of the row. Place the wire high enough so that it does not touch the tree plants.

Another method is to place tin cans every twelve to eighteen inches apart in your row with the tops and bottoms removed. Bury the bottom two inches of the can in the ground to keep it from falling over.

Melon and other vine crops, including beans, can be grown on metal fences, resulting in some of the most extraordinary results.

Whenever possible, use copper, which gives better results. For more information on the use of copper in gardening and farming you might write to Phelps Dodge Industries, 300 Park Avenue, New York, N.Y. Phelps Dodge is one of the largest copper companies in the world and is very promotion-minded and a strong proponent of gardening and growing to keep America beautiful.

Place a peony ring around your rose and see if you don't get a larger plant. Do the same for evergreens and shrubs to give them a better start.

To keep rabbits and other varmints away from your cabbage patch and charge the air at the same time, make a wire hut over your cabbage and other plants. This will keep your furry friends out and the electric energy in.

Tomatoes can be improved by training them to grow on metal poles rather than wooden stakes. Tie them with nylon strips made from discarded pantyhose.

Weeding

Grandma said that one of the surest signs that I had done a good job preparing the soil and helping to make it fertile was the army of hostile weeds that seemed to spring up overnight.

She said it was very important that I get them all up before they choke out the corn, peas, radish, and carrot seedlings. She also warned me how amazingly quickly weeds are able to go to seed.

She told me that old-fashioned farmers had trained geese to pull weeds, but the best and surest way to get rid of them is to get down on your hunkers or hands and knees and pull them with two hands. Pull weeds cautiously as you get close to each side of a row of vegetables. Too many folks get in too much of a hurry and pull up half of their crops along with the weeds. Be careful to pull them away from the young beets without disturbing their root hairs.

After you have cleaned up the rows by hand, go after the weeds between the rows. For this, you should use your hoe. Use a hand cultivator between rows of corn and potatoes. Run it up and down the rows, once in each direction.

Don't weed when the weather is wet and the ground is muddy. Unfortunately for you, hot, sunny days are the best ones for killing weeds. Weeding is one of the best ways I know to get a sunburn and a backache. Wear a hat and a neck bandana . . . and try not to kill yourself the first day. One good spring shower and you'll be surprised how quickly other weeds will grow to take their place. Don't get discouraged. If you stick it out you'll win the war, even if they do win a few battles.

Thinning

One of the worst mistakes that's made by new gardeners, as I was, is to allow vegetables to grow too close together . . . making them share the same soil and fight each other for the same nutrients.

When Grandma first sent me out to thin some of my crops, I was less than enthusiastic about pulling and discarding so many healthy-looking plants. I could just see my imagined profits flying away. Like most apprentice gardeners, I erred on the heavy side—leaving too many plants in each hill and row. What may look like plenty of room for several young seedlings to the inexperienced eye, will wind up being not at all enough when these plants are fully or even partially grown.

Be strong-minded—even heroic about thinning. Grandma said Indian women thinned their crops savagely. She may have meant that as a pun; but that's how you should do it, anyway.

As soon as a plant makes its second leaf, it needs your attention. Talk to it and give it a little encouragement during this early stage in its development. Look for the strongest and healthiest plants in a row or hill so you can spare most of them at thinning time.

Thinning should be done when the plants are "well up" and growing healthily. This usually means when there are three or four leaves on most of the plants in a particular stand. From these last two statements you can see that each kind of plant and each of its varieties may have a different growing and thinning schedule. Consult seed catalogs and seed packets for the proper time to thin your plants. Then, double-check to make sure they're "well up."

Some plants, like beets for instance, need two thinnings before the job is completed. In these cases, and whenever possible, cook and eat your thinnings instead of trying to transplant them.

Transplanting

If you begin growing your plants indoors, in a hot frame or a special outdoors seedbed, you will have to transplant them to the proper growing place in your garden.

Some plants that I have successfully transplanted include:

asparagus	lettuce
beets	onions
cabbage family	peppers
celery	potatoes
eggplant	radishes
kale	tomatoes

Other plants such as the legume family (peas, beans, etc.) and the cucurbits (squash, melons, etc.) can be transplanted if you do it very carefully. Be sure to move each plant with as large a ball of dirt around the roots as possible. Set a little deeper than it was planted before. Water after setting, firm the earth well, and if there is an especially hot sun, give your transplant some shade during the hottest part of the day. Do this for about a week or as long as the transplant shows any weakness.

Under normal circumstances you can, but will probably not want to, try to transplant corn or certain root crops like:

carrots	parsnips
garlic	sweet potatoes
Jerusalem artichokes	rutabagas
potatoes	turnips

Before transplanting, six or more leaves should be showing.

Blanching

Blanching is a garden operation designed to get rid of the green chlorophyll coloring of certain plants. This coloring comes from the sun during photosynthesis, so to get rid of it, simply block off the sun. To get rid of the green in:

asparagus: mound up the earth around the shoots or use boards to block out the sunlight.

cauliflower: tie up the leaves around the heart or flower.

celery: use boards, earth, large inverted clay pots, drain tile, or cardboard collars.

Other plants that are commonly blanched are sea kale and endive.

I don't believe in blanching because it's unnatural.

Easy Pickin' . . . Harvesting Your Vegetables

I think the best memories I have of growing that first garden with Grandma Putt, have to do with the cool part of the afternoon and early evening, just before suppertime.

That was the time of day we would take a deep old picnic basket with a lid on it and go out to the garden to pick our evening meal. Crisp leafy lettuce, crunchy carrots and radishes, bright red tomatoes, and tender string beans would join each other in the basket for the trip to the kitchen. Of course there was plenty of sampling done right on the spot. For a young boy, brushing the dirt off a fresh picked carrot and biting off a hunk has got to be one of the real delights of summer! Grandma always picked her vegetables during that part of the day or when it was cloudy and overcast.

In the case of sweet corn, she would have the water boiling before going out to pick it. She said the less time spent between the stalk and your mouth, the better the corn will taste. She was so right. Today, scientists tell me that an ear of corn begins losing its sugar about ten minutes after it's picked. That should make it pretty obvious that no corn you buy at a store or country stand will taste as good as the corn you grow in your own garden and eat immediately after picking.

Research also supports the custom of picking leafy vegetables in the evening. During the day, the sun burns up a lot of the vitamins and minerals stored in the plant leaves. As soon as the sun starts to set, the plants begin to replenish and refortify themselves.

Don't store vegetables in the hot sun after they've been picked. If you do, Old Sol will work hard and fast to diminish their nutritional value even after you've brought the vegetables out of the hot garden. Put them in the dark where it's cool. If you don't have a cool dark storage room or root cellar, use the basement laundry room or a dark corner of your garage. Wrap them in newspaper, cover them with clean straw, or, in the case of turnips, radishes, and carrots, in cool sand. Or keep them in a closed paper bag in the crisper drawer of your refrigerator.

Best of all, eat them right after you pick them! Try to avoid soaking your vegetables in cold water before cooking them. When you cook them, use as little water as possible and cook potatoes, carrots, beets, etc., with their jackets on. Most of the vitamins and minerals are in the skin or just under it. My friend Adelle Davis, gives lots of good tips in her books on preparing and cooking fresh vegetables. I don't agree with everything she says about growing vegetables entirely by organic methods, but she's a fine nutritionist and I endorse her tips on food preparation.

Talk To Your Plants

I can't believe you will be able to spend many hours in your garden before you will begin to talk to your plants.

Believe me, talking to vegetables, shrubs, grass, trees, and flowers is not a kooky or crazy thing to do. Getting to know each plant in your garden, personally, through good conversation, will help you become more observant of its general health and well-being.

By stopping to talk to a bean, a row of carrots, or a tomato plant, you may notice that one is beginning to yellow at the leaves, another needs thinning, and a third could use a little support.

Psychiatrists and psychologists have endorsed and recommended the therapeutic benefits of gardening for some time. Any doctor worth his degree will tell you that you're not a nut if you talk with the living, growing things in your garden.

Grandma said anyone who has been at gardening very long and very successfully, has become a great plant communicator. He is most likely reaping as much news from his garden as there is in the newspaper he uses for mulch.

So, if you want to have green-thumb success, get out there and start gabbing with your plants the minute they stick their heads above ground!

The "Compleat" Vegetable Gardener?

If you're anything like me, it will take you many, many growing seasons to become an accomplished gardener. Sometimes you will have a series of successful crops and harvests; at other times, you will find that you and Mother Earth are marching to the sounds of different drummers.

Like medicine or cooking, you never learn everything there is to know about gardening. There is no such guy or gal as "the compleat vegetable gardener." Gardening should be a labor of love. Each year, it should offer some new delights and new surprises. There will always be a new vegetable to try and grow or a new hybrid variety of one of the old standbys. Have fun; gardening is a pastime you should enjoy.

Here is a list of the most commonly grown vegetables. Good growing and good eating!

VEGETABLES

Asparagus	Mustard Greens
Beans	Okra
Beets	Onions
Brussels Sprouts	Orach
Cabbage	Parsley
Cauliflower	Peanuts
Celery	Peas
Chard	Peppers
Chives	Potatoes
Corn	Pumpkins
Cress	Radishes
Cucumbers	Red Cabbage
Eggplant	Rhubarb

Endive
Escarole
Globe Artichokes
Gourds
Jerusalem Artichokes
Kale
Kohlrabi
Leeks
Lentils
Lettuce
Muskmelon

Rutabagas
Savoy Cabbage
Spinach
New Zealand Spinach
Squash
Sweet Potatoes
Tomatoes
Strawberry Tomatoes
Turnips
Watermelon
Yams

A Vegetable Grower's Calendar

January—February—March:

1. In January, write for seed catalogs and nursery-stock offerings. That way, they'll come in plenty of time for you to sit down with paper and pencil and prepare this year's garden plan.

2. February is a good month to make sure your tools are clean and sharp. Now's the time to order and buy any new tools you may need. Check the supply of vegetables you stored, canned, or froze. Did you grow enough vegetables to keep you well-stocked? Did you overdo it? Make the proper adjustments in this year's plan.

3. In March, you can begin to start some seedlings indoors under glass. These will be for your early crops. The cabbage family, eggplants, asparagus, beets, the onion family, parsley, peppers, rhubarb, and tomatoes are most common indoor starters. You *can* start almost any plant indoors, but many have to be planted in individual biodegradable pots so that

they can be transplanted outdoors successfully. Sow fast growers four weeks before setting out, and slow growers up to eight weeks.

4. Don't rush into spring. Keep the plants you wintered over in the ground well mulched.

April—May—June

(Adjust these operations to local climate and weather):

1. If March was warm, and you didn't prepare your soil by ploughing deeply and manuring in the fall, perhaps early April is the time to do it. Dig up a spadeful of your soil and check its texture in your hands. If it crumbles easily and is not soggy, plowing or roto-tilling can begin. Set your blade for its deepest cut. Spade in gypsum, peat, manure, garden food, etc. (as described earlier).

2. If you did plow deeply in the fall, your garden should be easy to work. Set your roto-tiller for a depth of 6-10 inches. Reapply the gypsum, peat, manure, garden food, etc.

3. A week or two after tilling, check the soil and the temperature. If the last hard frost seems to have passed, and the days are sunny and warm, plant your early or cool season crops: asparagus, artichokes, rhubarb, lettuce, turnips, radishes, the cabbage family, etc.

4. Ten days to two weeks later, plant peas, corn, and beans. Don't be in a hurry to plant tomatoes and peppers. Hold them until late May or June. Grandma and her neighbors had

a tradition of planting pole beans after the longest day of the year—said they were better bearers and more disease resistant. My advice is to plant an early variety now, wait until June 22nd, then plant a second sowing. See which works best for you.

5. If there is a late frost warning, spread newspapers over your young shoots and take it off the next morning.

6. Catch the weeds before they get a good start. Water and fertilize regularly.

7. Thin your crops with determination. Make sure there's enough growing space between your plants on either side. Some crops like beets, require two thinnings. Eat the one you pull. Then when there are 3-4 leaves on your plants, they are "well up."

8. Transplant when there are 5-6 leaves. Be careful to give your transplants plenty of soil—a good-sized ball. Don't disturb the delicate root hairs.

July—August—September

1. In early July (or late June), plant your vegetables for an autumn harvest: eggplant, cabbage, melons, radishes, and pumpkins. Also, make second sowings of carrots, radishes, corn, beets, lettuce, and greens by the middle of the month.

2. When planting tomatoes, be sure to plant them deep enough so that the bottom row of leaves is flush with the ground. This assures a larger root system.

3. Watch out now for bugs and worms. Tomatoes and corn, America's two most popular home-garden crops, are highly susceptible. To a lesser degree, so are potatoes, peppers, and squash. Use the appropriate broad-spectrum control from the USDA approved list (pp. 38-40).

4. Don't overwater your garden during hot spells. Root rot may result. Water from below, not the tops of plants. Showers as described earlier in the chapter are prescribed from time to time.

5. Regular feedings with a 5-20-20 dry fertilizer and any of the fish emulsions is the best program.

6. Be on the lookout for blossom-end rot on the tomatoes. This occurs when the blossom-end of the tomato turns gray, then black. The disease is caused by poor distribution of moisture during hot weather. It's controlled by spraying with a solution of one tablespoon calcium chloride to a gallon of water.

7. Prop up tomatoes and pole beans. Staking will inhibit disease and insects. Try electroculture.

8. Prune tomatoes by pinching out the tops in late summer. This keeps them short and bushy. After the tomatoes bear fruit, pinch off the suckers. These worthless branches just eat and don't work—get rid of them!

9. Check the beets, carrots, parsnips, turnips, and other root crops for maggots. Spray the soil with 44% chlordane and they'll bug out.

10. If you used a newspaper mulch all spring and summer, you won't be troubled too much by weeds.

11. Most of your work from here on in will be picking beautiful vegetables. Don't let food go to waste. If you have too much, give it to neighbors and turn them on to gardening. When you harvest, the green tops from carrots, radishes, parsnips, and other root crops should be removed from the vegetables and left on the garden soil for green manure. Don't grind them up in the garbage disposal because their high nitrogen content will stimulate algae growth in our sewers and streams. Be pollution conscious in little ways.

October—November—December

1. Spade or plow up your garden in October. Add gypsum, manure, peat, garden food, etc. Leave all the vegetable foliage and green fruit. Plow it all under along with grass clippings and maple leaves. Ripe fruit and vegetables should be removed.

2. In November, add some late leaves to the vegetable garden. Just spread them out on top of the spaded or plowed soil.

3. In December, relax—you've been working too hard. If you feel extra ambitious, make some bird feeders for now and next spring.

Chapter 3.
Weeds
Worth Eating

Someone, my Uncle Art or Aunt Jane, had given me a jackknife for Christmas, but it wasn't until spring came and opened up my life to the outdoors that I really began to appreciate the wonders that could be wrought with this little gem of a tool!

Jackknives are good for playing mumbly-peg, the great sport of boys old enough to carry a "bone-handled, four-bladed pocket-equalizer." They are also good for cutting sticks, just in case you need a stick to carry with you on your travels. A man named Sam McGee, who ran the local filling station (he didn't sell much gas except for tractors in those war years), taught me how to whittle a wooden chain. Sam also kept the town fire engine at his garage. But since we didn't have more than one good barn fire every two or three years, he had time for lots of whittlin'—and teachin' of whittlin'.

Sam was absolutely nuts about fishing, as was my Uncle Art. It didn't take much persuading to get him to close down the station at noon on a summer Saturday and take us all down to the "crick," or better yet to the local river, which was about seven miles out in the country by Fowler's Woods.

First we'd drive down the hard road that ran through town, keeping our eyes peeled along either side of the roadway. Sure enough, we wouldn't have to go too many miles before we came across a dead chicken—killed by some truck that swooshed through our town without the driver even noticing he passed either one of the city limits.

Soon as we'd spot the dead bird, either Art or I would hop out of the car, grab up the bird, toss it on the fender of Sam's '36 Ford, and we'd be on our way again. When we got to the river bank, Sam would show me how to use my jackknife to open up the chicken to get at his intestines. At first I was a little squeamish about the operation, but after I saw how fast channel cats bite at bait made of little pieces of chicken guts or heart, I was well on my way to becoming the Dr. DeBakey of the Midwest.

It usually didn't take too long before we had several gunnysacks full of fish. Sometimes, if the afternoon was losing the sun, Sam would suggest cooking up a mess of fish right then and there.

Nothing tastes quite as good as fresh-caught fish pan-fried over an open fire—especially when you are half-dead from hunger (not having eaten since breakfast).

To go along with the fish, we sometimes brought a couple of potatoes to fry with the fish or bake in the ashes of the fire. If we forgot the spuds, Sam would take me for a short walk along the river or creek bank until we spied what he called "wild eatables." Once again, I'd get to use my new knife to harvest wild onions, asparagus, Indian potatoes, and, in the fall, pawpaws.

If we were really lucky, Art would wander up the other way and bring back a shirtful of wild blackberries or huckleberries. Fishin' with Sam McGee was always worth the trip—and we usually went home with our bags full of fish and our bellies full of food.

Wild Eatables

Just turn a small boy loose in a field or woods where there are green apple trees or wild huckleberry bushes and you will discover traces of that insatiable inquiring appetite that got Adam into so much trouble in Eden. A ten-year-old boy with a sharp knife will eat (and sometimes overeat) just about anything! This often results in what my Grandma Putt called "The Green Apple Quick-Step." But most of the time, she didn't seem to mind ministering to my bellyaches. As a matter of fact, Grandma encouraged me to taste almost everything growing wild in the vicinity of her place.

She said too many mothers recoil in needless horror over the thought of their young sons unleashing their appetites in the "wilds" of North America.

"Once you get to know poison ivy and its brother, poison oak, there aren't too many plant people in the woods you need to fear tasting. If a plant tastes too bitter, acid or sour, just spit it out. If you find something that looks good enough to eat and you're not sure—especially a member of the mushroom family—bring it home . . . and maybe I'll know what it is."

That kind of encouragement was all I needed to become an eager forager and explorer of Mother Nature's boy-ways.

In the fields and woods, I quickly learned some more about the subtle relationships and interactions between plants, animals, and humans. How they help each other to survive and propagate.

Speaking of propagation, on a good day's jaunt, blowing dandelion parachutes, carrying cockleburs on my pants, shaking nuts and other fruits from trees, "thinning" the wild berry crops, and robbing honey from a wild bees nest—I probably accomplished more for plant reproduction than Luther Burbank!

I also learned that Mother Nature takes care of her own. That some plants didn't need any help from me. I saw the violets and the touch-me-nots were able to shoot their own seeds some distance. That watercress had only to release a few stems and they would soon find a new place to root and grow a little distance downstream.

I learned that the greatest danger to my safety and well-being in the woods or along the creek came just at dusk. That was when the mosquitoes appeared to drink my blood. Grandma made up one of her Indian recipes containing several herbs with citronella and my mosquito scars and chigger bites were reduced dramatically. Sam McGee would often get a small bottle of Grandma's mosquito repellent to take along on our fishing expeditions. He said that since it was the female mosquitoes that caused all the trouble, it was only right that a woman should brew up the repellent. Uncle Art would carry a carbide lamp if we ever went "froggin' " after dark. The burning carbide must have smelled better to the "skeeters" than it did to me because they came in droves to be burned to a crisp.

During the day, when I was on my own catching grass-hoppers or chasing butterflies, I would find all sorts of plant specimens to gather for food or bring home to have identified. Here is a list of some of them.

A Boy's Guide to Wild Eatables (Weeds and Such)

Wild onions . . . the bulbs are tough, but take them home to flavor the soup.

Peppermint . . . you'll probably disregard my advice about the wild onions anyway, so eat some peppermint leaves to hide the smell. Or, bring them home for peppermint tea.

Groundnuts (Indian potatoes) . . . look for the purple-brown flowers and twining vines. The older plants will have the largest tubers. They're good for eating raw, frying, baking, and roasting.

Asparagus . . . make a sack out of your shirt, snap off the young stalks and carry as many home as you can. You'll be a hero at suppertime!

Jack-in-the-pulpit . . . Grandma said the Indians boiled and ate the roots. (Be careful, other parts are poisonous.) But, after a couple of tries eating both young and older plant roots, I began to pass them by. Try boiling some (change the water at least twice to get the acid out) and see what you think.

Skunk cabbage . . . believe it or not, this foul-smelling plant can be delicious (change the water when you boil it).

Dandelions . . . they're best taken from an open field where they grow wild.

Jerusalem artichokes . . . they look like hairy sunflowers. When you spot some, remember where they're located. In the fall, dig up the tubers—they're better than potatoes.

Chicory . . . some states have laws about picking wildflowers along the roadways. If your doesn't, chicory is great to spice up a salad or to dry and grind the roots to brew with coffee.

Catalpa trees . . . nothing there worth eating, but I've smoked many catalpa cigars as a boy and think they're much more fun than cornsilk.

Honey locust trees . . . Grandma showed me the sweet pulp between the seed pods . . . she said these were the "locusts" John the Baptist ate. (Some black locusts are poisonous).

Persimmon . . . don't try 'em when they're not ripe or you'll be puckered up for a week!

Pokeweed . . . you'll find it along some fence, or growing as a weed in the spring-spaded soil of your garden. Grandma used the shoots for potherbs, I used the berries for "ink" to write secret messages. Don't eat the roots, they're poisonous.

May apples (American Mandrake) . . . you'll smell them before you see them. The plants have a two-inch white flower and a big, single leaf. They appear in early spring, but the fruit (which look like small, gold eggs) aren't any good until July or August when they're golden-yellow.

Pawpaws . . . grow on trees, mostly in thickets. You'll have to acquire a taste for the fruit. They look like short stubby bananas.

Other good-eating things (some, I never tried) were: bark from sassafras trees for tea, elder leaves for cough syrup, daylily bulbs (which you can use today in Chinese cooking), sweet flag for calamus candy, wild spinach, bloodroot, horseradish, black mustard, sunflowers, wild rice, golden thistle nettles, chickweed, wake robin, Solomon's seal, slippery elm for chewing, field sorrel, cheeses (mallows), Johnny jumpups, cowslips and on and on and on. . . .

Walking along the gravel road toward the woods one summer day, I came across some scatterings of big white flowers with maroonish-looking eyes. Thinking they were wild morning glories, I picked as many as I could and brought them home to Grandma. She told me to get the vegetable fork and a gunnysack from the shed and show her where I had found the flowers. When we came to the flower field, she had me dig in the dry soil below one of the plants, for its root. Before long, I had unearthed a huge root as big around as my thigh and about a foot and a half long! Grandma said the Indians called these plants man-in-the-earth and that they roasted the roots or boiled them. I wanted to take the big root home for cooking, but she advised me to look for a younger plant with a smaller tap-root.

We had some boiled man-in-the-earth that evening. But even though Grandma had changed the water several times when she cooked it, I found it somewhat bitter-tasting, like some turnips. (I love turnips now, but at ten, they weren't my favorite vegetables.) I remember eating "the whole thing" very manfully except for a taste I gave my Aunt Jane, who wrinkled up her nose and said it tasted too strong.

Ginger (American wild ginger, that is) was another wild herb we gathered in the woods. A little bit of the ground root of this plant goes a long way. Grandma used ginger in her "medicines," but she had another use for it that I preferred a whole lot more.

Root Beer

Going out with Grandma to pick the roots and bark for root beer, was one of the best adventures of spring! We would criss-cross the fields that skirted the woods, our eyes peeled sharp. Grandma carried a garden trowel, I had my trusty jackknife and an old flour sack. This is what we looked for:

Dandelion roots, burdock and yellow-dock roots. The bark of the wild cherry and some birchbark. Then we scouted the fields until we found elecampane, sarsaparilla, and spikenard.

Up in Grandma's hot attic, she had a small gunnysack full of hops that had been hanging there to dry since last autumn.

HOW TO MAKE "GRAM'S OLD-FASHIONED ROOT BEER"

Here is the recipe for Grandma's Root Beer. This will make two gallons:

Ingredients

    1 oz. burdock roots
    1 oz. dandelion roots
    1 oz. yellow-dock roots
    1 oz. elecampane roots
    1 oz. sarsaparilla roots
    1 oz. spikenard roots

    1 oz. wild cherry bark
    1 oz. birchbark
    1 oz. hops

    2 gallons cold water in a large kettle

    1 lb. sugar
    25 drops oil of sassafras or spruce
    8 tbls. liquid yeast, or a dry yeast cake dissolved in a cup of tepid water.

Directions

1. Wash roots and bark very clean. Then, bruise them so the oils and juices will cook out easily.

2. Put cold water into a cleanly scoured kettle. Add your roots etc., and bring to a slow boil.

3. Simmer for about half an hour. Toward the end of the half hour, add your sugar and 20 to 25 drops of the oil of sassafras or spruce.

4. Put slowly into an earthen crock and cool to lukewarm.

5. Add the yeast. Stir it in, cover, and set it away to ferment.

6. It will be drinkable in from three to six hours. Or seal and store. Fermented, the beverage is slightly alcoholic and very delicious!

There are literally thousands of plants worth looking at, talking to, and eating, within walking distance of your home whether you live in the city or out in the country like Grandma Putt.

There are also many other good reasons to take nature rambles than just to heal your body or feed your appetite. And, there are plenty of plants worth talking to just to find out what they are like and what they are up to. One of these is mistletoe.

Mistletoe, Parasites, and Plants of the Forest

The ancient Druids and other northern Europeans had a special reverence for mistletoe. Probably, because it was one of the few plants to keep some green to it during the winter. Imagine those old Druids looking up at a leafless tree in the dead of winter and seeing a two or three foot *green* batch of mistletoe growing out of one of the limbs!

Actually, mistletoe is a partial parasite whose seed is carried up onto the limbs of trees by birds who have just dined on their sticky pale-white berries. There was plenty of mistletoe growing in the trees around Grandma's, and drinking up their sap. Any boy looks for a reason to climb trees, and collecting mistletoe is still one of the best ones ever!

There are several plants which take their meals at the expense of other living plants. You are likely to come across some of these not far from your home or in local forest preserves, woods, and parks. Among these are the dodder, beechdrops, and the Indian paintbrush and fungi.

Then too, you will want to take a good look at the bracket fungus which grows up and down the trunks of huge trees literally eating away at its host's innards.

If you live in the southeastern part of the United States, you will be acquainted with Spanish moss, which can be seen hanging from the trees arching most streets. This plant is epiphytic, an air plant; it grows on trees, other plants, and on wires and posts, but makes its own food from the atmosphere, rain, and debris around it, not drawing on its host at all. Spanish moss is not a true moss, anyway—it belongs to the pineapple family!

Orchids, among the most beautiful and dramatic plants of the tropics, are also air plants, although they are often mistakenly called parasites. Among the 800 varieties of orchids, there are a number that are rooted in the earth as well. Don't let anyone tell you that you can't find orchids growing wild in the United States; there are plenty of them in Hawaii. One or two orchid varieties grown in Mexico are not much for their flowers, but they supply about 90 percent of all the vanilla that's used in world commerce. If you picked a vanilla bean off one of these plants and tasted it, you would find no hint of the vanilla taste that's so familiar to all of us. How ancient Indian tribes of Mexico discovered and developed the very complicated process of drying, aging, and preparing the seeds is one of the great plant mysteries of all time.

Mushrooms and Toadstools . . .
Some Worth Eating, All Worth Watching

In your garden you will come up against certain fungi that are worth watching and eliminating. The word *fungus* gives some folks the shudders and makes them run for their fungicide and sprayers. And no wonder, too; these parasite fungi include "bad guys" like potato blight, wheat rust and the *real bad guys* that cause diphtheria and typhoid fever in people and animals.

But out in the woods you will find fungi which are not parasites. They are hard workers for Mother Nature and Mother Earth because they live and feed off dead and decaying matter like fallen branches and tree stumps. They help speed up the decaying process and return valuable minerals to the soil. Among these are the plants we know as mushrooms and toadstools.

I found plenty of these in the woods and near the creek by Grandma's. They are especially plentiful all summer when there is a warm, wet spring. Grandma said God provided for small boys by making them dislike mushrooms, and I think she was right. Loving them as I do now, I really feel nostalgic twinges of regret that I didn't harvest any of the thousands I saw that summer.

Once in a while, Grandma would go with me to gather mushrooms and she'd fill a bag to overflowing. That night, all the adults would be oohing and ahing over sliced fresh mushrooms sauteed in herb butter. I wish I could spend some of those dinnertimes over again now! It seems all wrong to have missed out on enjoying some of the very best "wild eatables." Why don't you get a book or guide without delay so you can begin learning which of the mushrooms are poisonous "toadstools" and which are among Mother Earth's finest delicacies for cooking and eating raw. Don't put your faith in old wives' tales that claim to show which species are poisonous. (No, poisonous mushrooms *don't* turn silver spoons black). The best way to get a treat instead of a treatment is to study, carefully, which ones are good eating.

Once again, use a book with accurate photographs or illustrations. Or take along a knowledgeable guide who had been gathering and eating mushrooms from the wild for many years.

Why You Should Go Into the Woods and Fields

Besides their fascination for youngsters and curious adults, the wild plants that you will find in the fields and woods have been, and can be, put to many uses that benefit man. It's amazing what we can learn from even the lowliest weed.

The Milkweed

For example, take the common milkweed that many gardeners have been hoeing and weeding from their flower beds and vegetable patches for years. The young shoots or stalks of this plant can be boiled and eaten like asparagus, and are about as tasty a vegetable dish as you will ever set on your table. The Indians also cooked and ate the buds, pods and roots of milkweed. If you try cooking milkweed, don't forget to change your water two or three times as the plants will turn out to be bitter if you don't. (There are three poisonous varieties of milkweed which grow in the south. Check these out before you eat any). Like most youngsters, I was curious to see the "milk" that gives this plant its name. So, Grandma broke a stem and the sticky milky substance gushed out. She said this is not the sap, but a special "juice" or secretion which the plant uses to heal itself when its stems are partially cut or broken.

During WW II, the government found two additional uses for milkweed: as the stuffing for Navy life preservers and in the linings of Army Air Force flight jackets. Government scientists discovered that the milkweed silk was more bouy-ant than cork and several times less heavy, but just as warm, as wool. This common weed may be credited with saving countless lives.

Children Make Great "Weeders-of-the-Woods!"

There are many helpful and curious plant-people growing in the wild. For some you will have to search in the local woods, or near swamps. Others you will find along railroad right-of-ways, roadsides, and river banks. Take along some kids, either your own or a few from the neighborhood. Taking nature walks to search for "plant strangers" can pay off in countless human rewards for all of you—including good eating!

A Sweet Afterthought

One kind of natural food that you and your young friends may come across on your nature walks is wild honey.

While honey isn't exactly a plant food, it is a by-product of plant reproduction. As the bees move from blossom to blossom to drink the nectar and gather "bee glue" from the trees, shrubs, and wild flowers in the fields and woods, they carry pollen with them. At each blossom, some of this pollen is accidentally left behind so the plant can reproduce.

HONEY BEES

When I lived at Grandma Putt's, I learned to tell the difference between plain old bees and "honey bees." Most bees only drink the nectar from the flowers. Honey bees take it back to their hive and store it. The familiar bumblebees are one of the few species of native North American honey bees. The small honey bees you see swarming around some hollow log in the woods are probably descendants of bees that were introduced by the very first colonists to this country.

FOLLOWING A "BEE-LINE"

Grandma used honey for many of her "medicines" and for cooking. She showed me how to make a "bee-line box" so I could follow the bees to their hive. Take an old wooden matchbox. Fill it with cornstarch or cornmeal soaked in honey-water. Set it in a conspicuous spot near where you see some bees working on flowers. As the bees come again and again to the box, they will pick up some of the color of the cornstarch. You can follow the "colored" bees home. Keep moving the box in the direction they are flying.

You'll be surprised to find how far bees will go from their hives in search of nectar. You'll have to be very patient in tracking them. You will also find that they are very sneaky about how they enter their hive, so be alert and observant!

REMOVING THE HONEY

If you are extremely sensitive to insect bites and bee stings, leave the gathering of honey to someone who knows what he is doing. A man named Roy States who lived near Grandma kept honey bees in his orchard. Any good orchard-man or flower gardener will tell you how valuable bees are to his success. Mr. States had a standing offer of one dollar for any good-sized swarm of bees I could find for him. He would transfer the swarm to one of his hives, and Grandma and I would get the wild honey. Mr. States said that bees normally won't sting when they are swarming, but I can remember standing well clear when he was working.

A Wild-Weed Hunter's Calendar

Here is a list of the tasty treats a wild-weed hunter will find in the fields and woods near his home. It is by no means complete. And, I have saved most berries, fruits, and nuts for later chapters.

EARLY SPRING

*Leaves
  and Shoots:*
Asparagus
Blue Violet
Burdock
Burnet
Cattails
Chickweed
Chicory
Marsh Cress

Skunk Cabbage
Wake Robin
Yellow-dock

Roots:
Arrowhead
Bloodroot
Wild Garlic
Wild Ginger
Wild Onion

Winter Cress
Dandelion
Marsh Marigold
New Jersey Tea Plant
Penny Cress
Pokeweed
Shepherd's Purse
Spicebush
Spruce

Sweet Flag
Valerian

Barks:
Birch bark
Sassafras
Slippery Elm
Spicebush
Spruce

MID-SPRING TO MID-SUMMER

Leaves
  and Shoots:
Burdock
Burnet
Cattails
Red Clover
Century Plant
  (Southwest, West)
Corn Salad
Bitter Cress
Watercress
Elecampane
Fennel
Good King Henry
Horehound
Lady's Thumb
Lamb's Quarter
Prickly Lettuce
Wild Lettuce
Mallow (Cheeses)
Milkweed
Stinging Nettles
Wood Nettles
Pigweed
Plantain
Peppergrass

Purslane
Indian Rhubarb
Touch-Me-Not
Wood Sorrel

Roots:
Wild Garlic
Wild Ginger
Groundnuts (Indian Potatoes)
Horseradish
Jack-In-The-Pulpit
Wild Licorice
Wild Potatoes
Salsify
Sweet Myrrh
Valerian

Flavorings:
Spicebush
Birchbark
New Jersey Tea Plant
Sassafras
Sweet Gum

Fruit:
May Apples

LATE SUMMER AND AUTUMN

Leaves, Stalks
  and Shoots:
Cattails
Catnip

Prairie Apples
  (Midwest to Rockies)
Marsh Mallow

Watercress
Mallow
Purslane
Sugar Cane

Seeds and Pods:
Wild Beans
Black Mustard
Wild Buckwheat
Wild Oats
Wild Rice
Wild Wheat
Sunflower Seeds
Honey Locust Pods
Locust Pods

Roots:
Arrowhead
Cattails
Daylilies
Wild Ginger
Groundnuts
Horseradish
Jerusalem
  Artichokes

Fruit:
Ground Cherries
May Apples
Pawpaws
Persimmons

Beverages and
  Flavorings:
Balsam
Bee Balm
Birchbark
Sweet Bay
Box Elder
Hemlock
Horse Gentian
Kentucky Coffee Tree
Lemon Balm
Wild Mint
New Jersey Tea Plant
Peppermint
Sassafras
Spearmint
Spruce
Sumac
Sweet Gale

WINTER TO EARLY SPRING

This time of year in the North and East, there's not much growing. Some roots are available if you can find them. Also fruits, etc. Just enjoy a walk in the winter wonderland. If you live in the South and Southwest, you'll be gathering wild foods all year round.

Chapter 4.
Herbs
Worth Growing

The Search

Since the dawn of pre-history, curious and enterprising people like my Grandma Putt have been going into the fields and woods to search for plants. The plants they were seeking were not just to be used as food. Some of them were gathered for their medicinal value. Others, for the spices and flavorings and beverages they added to improve the taste and quality of simple meals of meat and vegetables.

Gradually, these exotic herbs were brought under cultivation and came into general use. Some, which were indigenous to a specific locality, were carried nearly around the world in caravans and caravels. And, it was the search for these herbs and spices—as much as the lure of gold—which sent explorers and adventurers on voyages of discovery to Africa, Asia, and the Americas.

To a medieval Europe, where meat was slaughtered in the fall and was pretty well spoiled by Christmas, many of the plant foods we take for granted, like pepper, sugar, cloves, cinnamon, coffee, and tea were an overnight eating and drinking sensation! Before their discovery, it was the custom

105

to try to prevent the putrefaction of meat with generous applications of herbs which were grown locally. An herb garden was an important feature of any European home.

In addition to their help as food flavorings and perfumes, herbs were discovered to have healing powers long before men learned to read and write. Grandma, who had read her Bible hundreds of times, was familiar with the herbs mentioned there and their uses. Many of the herb remedies still used by simple folk and doctors and pharmacists, can be traced back to the time of the Romans, Greeks, Egyptians, and Hebrews. And we owe an enormous debt of gratitude to the Arabs, Africans, Asians, and Indians of North and South America for the thousands of medicines they developed from local growing plants. Sure, many times these folk medicines were discarded or abandoned as newer ones came along. However, it's surprising how often the properties discerned in them by simple and even savage herb doctors have been rediscovered and developed by modern medical researchers.

My friend, Victor Sen Yung, whom many of you used to know as the irascible Chinese cook on the television program, "Bonanza," tells me about a plant called *ma huang* which has been used for more than five thousand years in China in the treatment of hay fever. In the last twenty or thirty years, scientists have extracted a valuable alkaloid, *ephedrene,* which is currently used in the treatment of asthma. The ancient Chinese believed that the *ma huang* should be gathered in the fall, and modern research backs this up too. Chemical analysis shows that the ephedrene content increases in the fall to nearly two hundred percent more than the plant contains in the spring. No wonder modern medicine doesn't laugh at all the herb medicine practices of the ancients!

I think it's safe to say that all peoples, everywhere—no matter what stage of civilization they're in—have gathered and cultivated herbs. There are hundreds of herbs used by people the world over, the list is almost endless. Most Americans these days buy dried and powdered herbs which are cultivated, prepared, and sold commercially. But, if you want my opinion, few if any have the taste and fragrance of fresh herbs.

Spicy Ladies?

Many people ask me the difference between *herbs* and *spices*. Well, I'm no expert, so I asked my friend Joe Daley, who has just completed a kitchen-centered horror story *(Spicy Lady)*, to help me out. He has kindly consented to share some of his spicy research and sage observations.

Joe says that American wives have a questionable tradition of being heavy-handed with the spice shakers. To back this claim, he cites the 100,000,000 pounds of spices consumed in this country every year! When you realize that most of the spices sold in the United States come in tiny boxes or bottles, you've got to go along with him.

The spices most of us know and use are "the classic spices" of ancient times and the age of discovery. These include: *allspice,* which Columbus discovered growing on trees in Jamaica and promptly mislabeled "pimiento"; *bay* which comes from the leaves of the Greek's sacred laurel trees and shrubs. (The oil of bay was mixed with alcohol in the West Indies and was promptly labeled "Bay rum"); *capers,* which grow on bushes on the shores of the Mediterranean Sea; *capsicum,* a number of South and Central American peppers the most important of which is *cayenne pepper; cardamon,* used in sausage-making and curry powders, these hot seeds came originally from India; *eassia,* what most of us know as cinnamon is mentioned several times in the Old Testament; *cinnamon,* probably came from China, and is mentioned in

The Thousand and One Nights, which says Sinbad made a fortune by bringing cinnamon to Baghdad (In another part of that book, he used the spice as an aphrodisiac—one of the first spicy books!); *clove,* which the Chinese courtiers used in ancient times to put in their mouth to sweeten their breath before an audience with the emperor; *ginger,* also from China. We use it in our nonalcoholic ginger ale, and the British in their slightly fermented ginger beer; *mace and nutmeg,* from the "spice islands" of Indonesia. Both from the same tree (Polite and cultured ladies used to carry dainty little nutmeg cases and tiny grinders to help flavor their booze); *paprika,* from Central America and India and great on Welsh rabbit; *tumeric,* now grown in Indonesia, it was mentioned often in the Bible and is one of the main ingredients in curry powder; *saffron,* the costliest spice of all . . . it takes about a quarter of a million hand-picked stamens of the autumn crocus to make a pound, which sells for about four dollars; *sesame seed,* from China, used in cooking and medicine. Another spice I almost forgot is *mustard*—both black and white mustard are grown principally for their seed and are native to Europe and Asia Minor. The seeds are ground and are the main ingredient in prepared mustard. You can grow it here if you live in the west.

Curry powder must also be included in the spice list. This complicated mixture of dried herbs and spices has been traced as far back as the ancient city-state of the Indian subcontinent, Mohenjo-Daro. This is one of the cradles of civilization and was unearthed only about a half-century ago. It is located in Pakistan near the Indus river, and is one of the earliest civilizations known to archeologists. The people who lived there, about 2500-1500 B.C. seem to have discovered and developed rice. (And what good is rice without curry powder some will ask?) As far as we know they were the first to season foods, and may have invented the mortar and pestle to crush and blend spices. The curry powder we buy today is a secret blending, but most experts believe it contains: allspice, cardamon, coriander, cumin, fennel, fenugreek, and tumeric.

It may be hard for you to believe it, but great wars were fought over spices, great discoveries were made because of them, and great countries rose or fell by controlling them. The average American housewife today has more spices on her pantry shelves or spice racks than some of the wealthiest kings of ancient times or of Europe in the Middle Ages!

Herbs

Technically, herbs are all the remaining plants which can't be classified as trees or shrubs. Obviously, that includes an enormous group of flowers, vegetables, and weeds. In more general use, herbs (commonly pronounced in the U.S. with the "h" sounded) is a term applied to plants used as aromatics. They can be used as food flavorings, beverages, deodorizers, and pesticides. The list is practically endless, the herbs in common usage really depends on where you happen to live. Here is the best list I could assemble using several sources. It is by no means complete:

COMMON, AND NOT-SO-COMMON, HERBS

ambrosia	lemon verbena
angelica	lesser-leaved garlic
anise	licorice
arnica	lovage
balm	marigold
basil,	marjoram,
sweet	sweet
dwarf	wild
Italian	May apple (American
lemon	mandrake)

bay
betony
wood betony
Paul's betony
borage
burdock
burnet
calamus
caraway
castor oil plant
catnip
celeriac
celery
chamomile
chervil
chicory
chives
clary sage
colewort
coriander
costmary
cresses,
  upland
  garden
  water
cumin
dill
fennel,
  wild
  sweet
  carosella
fennel flower
fenugreek
feverfew
foxglove
fumitory
garlic
gentian
geranium,
  rose
  white (lemon)
germander
good King Henry

mint,
  apple
  berganmot
  curley
  pennyroyal
  peppermint
  spearmint
mugwort
nasturtium
nightshade,
  black-berried
  malabar (white)
oregano
parsley
pepper,
  Tabasco
  chili
plantain
poppy
purslane
rhubarb
rocambole
rose,
  damask
  cabbage
  China
  sweetbrier
rosemary
rue
sage
santolinas,
  lavender cotton
  emerald green
smallage
samphire
savory,
  summer
  winter
shallot
sorrel,
  French
  garden
  wood

hellebore
hemlock
henbane
hop
horehound
horseradish
hyssop
lamb's quarter (pigweed)
lavender
leek

sweet Cicely
sweet woodruff
tansy
tarragon
thyme,
  wild
  garden
wasabi (Japanese horseradish)
wormwood
yarrow

Cures and Cure-Alls

At one time or other, almost every herb listed above was used in folk or herb medicine. Of course, there are thousands and thousands more which space, or lack of it, won't allow listing.

Grandma Putt was a great believer in some of the medicinal properties of both European and American herbs . . . and other plants, including: wild-apple cider and apple-cider vinegar for aches and pains; blackberry leaves as tea or blackberry brandy for intestinal problems; burdock root ground up, for skin problems; cabbage leaves for drunkenness; castor-oil plant internally for the stomach and externally for warts and pimples; cinnamon tea in the wintertime as a preventive; chickweed tea as a purgatory; chamomile tea for stomach cramps and menstrual cramps. . . also for colds which settle in the stomach; wild cherries in cough syrup; dill applied to the skin to leech out infection; feverfew . . . for what the name implies; horehound for sore throat; foxglove for heart pains; hawthorn haws brewed into a heart-toner; juniper berries as a tea for colds; knotweed . . . the root contains tannic acid; licorice for sore throat, ulcers, and chronic skin problems; mustard for mustard plasters; nettles in tonic; plantation tea for just about everything; pennyroyal

111

in teas; rose teas; sarsaparilla as a female's change-of-life tonic; strawberry leaves for indigestion; tansy to purify the blood; touch-me-not for rubbing on mosquito bites; valerian for nerves (it was used in WW I to treat shell-shock); wintergreen for teas and in liniment; witch hazel; yarrow in tonics. She believed in using honey with herbs and the old apple-a-day saying. Grandma said that it was a shame that the medicines of the Indians were mostly lost or perverted. That, actually, the Indians were way ahead of the shoddy kind of medicine practiced by the first white settlers in this country who held to the belief in what was called "The Doctrine of Signatures." This doctrine said that whatever a plant looked like, that was the ailment it was good for . . . an herb like eyesbright, was used for eye ailments because it was white with a dark, pupil-like spot on the flower, resembling an eye; lungwort, whose leaves were spotted, was used for treatment of lung ailments; etc., etc.

The Indians were very good with poultices and salves. They helped the settlers pull through many a fever and recover from many a wound. Grandma said that when she was a girl, and in Great-Grandpa Coolidge's time, the entire United States was filled with phony Indian medicine men and gypsy caravans, all peddling worthless "Indian" remedies. These cure-alls were supposed to be good for anything that ailed you, but you were taking your health in your hands if you drank the horrible-tasting stuff.

I remember coming home once and telling Grandma that Tommy Rawlins had come to school with the measles. She made me sit down right then at the kitchen table to drink some wild ginger tea and eat a molasses cookie. In a half hour, I had sweated out my measles!

Grandma's Herb Garden

Grandma Putt had herbs growing all over her place. Some were in the vegetable patch and others were in the fields and wood nearby. But most of her fragrant and kitchen herbs were to be found in a little four-by-four-foot plot just beneath her kitchen window. It was edged with strawberry plants and I remember that she used the strawberry leaves in her salads from time to time.

How to Grow an Herb Garden of Your Own

Many herb gardeners like to lay out their plot in a formal or geometric pattern. Use your creative powers and do what suits you. Like every other kind of gardening, start your herb garden with just a few specimens of a kind. Plant them in a protected spot, in full sun. Some old-timers will tell you that herbs don't need good soil to grow well. My advice is to plant them in the best-drained, most fertile soil you have on your property. They like sandy, alkaline soil that's friable. Don't overwater, they can take dry spells very well. Also, don't worry about diseases, their natural oils and aromas keep most bugs away. Feed them only sparingly.

Herbs grow slowly, so you may want to start them indoors on a sunny windowsill. Then, set them out after the danger of frost is past. Keep the taller perennials at the back of your herb garden: hyssop, tarragon, sage, etc. Don't forget to save some room for annuals like: borage, basil, marjoram, savory, dill, etc. Parsley is another good edging plant for your herb garden. For fragrance add lavender, clove, nutmeg, lemon crispum, etc. For color, roses.

Other Ways to Grow Herbs

Window boxes make very acceptable herb gardens. Use four-inch pots side by side on a tray outside your kitchen window. Keep water in the tray, but don't let it be in contact with your potted herbs. When the soil is dry, place each pot in water until the soil is saturated. Use chives, dill, tarragon, chervil, thyme, mint, and parsley.

Yard and Fruit Magazine suggests growing herbs in a strawberry jar, or Mexican olla. These pots are about eighteen inches in diameter and three feet tall with openings all around the sides. Use each of these openings as a home for one of your herbs.

Here's how to prepare the herb pot: Mix two parts good garden soil or planter's mix with one part each of steer manure and gypsum and peat moss. Make a center core of gravel surrounded by wire mesh and fill in your soil mixture around that core. Water daily. You can keep the jar on a sunny patio or porch or apartment terrace. You should end up with lots of herbs for friends and neighbors.

Herbs can be planted as borders along walks, in hanging baskets, in wooden tubs, in the hollow centers of concrete blocks or in individual pots.

If you don't have the room or yen for any of the above, mix your herbs in with your bed of flowers or vegetables. You won't be sorry . . . they'll spice up your garden and your life!

Using Your Herbs

One good thing to remember *before* you use your herbs is that dried herbs are much stronger and "more insistent" than fresh ones. Use about a half to one-third dried as you would fresh.

Fresh Herbs

You can pick leaves or sprigs from culinary herbs like basil, dill, chives, mints, parsley, etc., while they are growing. Gather them when they've grown large enough to stand the shock of removing part of their foliage. Pinching off what you need for your salads or seasonings will stimulate more branching and new growth.

Herb Seeds

Allow the herbs you are growing for seeds to flower. The time to harvest herb seeds like anise and caraway is when the seed heads turn brown and just before they drop their seed.

Drying Herbs

Since many herbs are annuals, and will be through by fall, you will want to learn the useful procedure of drying and preserving them.

There is a right way and a wrong way to dry herbs. Don't cut and dry them in the sun because you will dry out the herb's peculiar oil or fragrance. Another bad move is to tie them up under some kind of cover. This may cause them to discolor, get moldy, or ferment.

The right way to dry herbs is to gather them as soon as they begin to open their flowers. Be sure that they are dry, and not moist, when you cut or pick them. Be sure to brush off any dirt and pick off any dead leaves. Hang them in some old nylon stockings or pantyhose so that the air can get at them from all sides. After they are entirely dry, put them in paper bags, and write in crayon the name of the herb and the date you tied it up. If you prefer, you can put them in decorative bottles or jars with airtight stoppers. Grandma had a special shelf for these herbs in her kitchen pantry, and their mixture of pungent and subtle fragrances (along with a large supply of molasses and sugar cookies), made it a great place to visit!

Some herbs, such as basil, burnet, fennel, etc., lose their fragrance when they are dried. You might try keeping them in paper or plastic bags in the crisper compartment of your refrigerator. And although some experts will disagree, Ilene has successfully frozen some of our herbs without any loss of their special qualities. Just rinse them off with cold water and allow to dry in a colander. Place them in plastic bags with a card for identification and put them in the freezer or freezing compartment.

Poundin' and Squeezin'

Something you might want to try is extracting oils from fresh herbs and making powders out of dry ones. For these operations, you will need an extracter and a mortar and pestle. You can consult your druggist, or contact the Herb Society of America (510 Gettysburg St., Pittsburgh, Pennsylvania 15206), to find out where these tools might be available in your area.

Keep juices and oils of mints, spruce, sassafras, etc., in airtight bottles. Powdered herbs can be kept in jars and bottles. Good sealing will insure freshness.

An Herb Grower's Planting Calendar

Herbs such as lemon balm, dandelion, lovage, marjoram and rosemary, which are perennials in the south, should be

116

treated as annuals in the cold northern regions of the country. If possible, northern gardeners should start herbs indoors on sunny windowsills. Put them out well after the last frost and take them in again in the fall. Remember, most herbs are slow growers. Grow herbs using the same vegetable-gardening techniques as outlined in Chapter II. Since you will want only a few specimens of each, many herbs are best purchased from an herb nursery rather than grown from seed.

SPRING:

Angelica seed should be sown in early spring. Also:

Anise	Germander
Betony	Horehound
(all types)	Hyssop
Borage	Lavender
Burnet	Leek
Catnip	Pot Marigold
Chamomile	Sweet Marjoram
Chicory	Black Mustard
Clary	White Mustard
Coriander	Nasturtium
Cresses	Poppy
Cumin	Rosemary
Dandelion	Rue
(pick wild)	Summer Savory
Fennel Flower	Winter Savory

You can plant bergamot root divisions in early spring. Also:

Lemon Balm	Germander (set plants)
(roots and cuttings)	Horseradish (roots)
Betony (set plants)	Hyssop (seedlings)
Burdock (pick wild)	Lemon Verbena
Catnip	(seedlings)
Chamomile	Spearmint (set plants)
(set plants)	Rhubarb (root crowns)
Chives (bulbs)	Rocambole (set plants)
Comfrey (roots)	Roses (set plants)

117

Costmary (set plants)
Dill (set plants)
Feverfew
  (root division)
Garlic (bulbs)
Geraniums (set plants)

Winter Savory
  (root division)
Shallot (bulbs)
Tansy (root division)
Mock or Wild Ginger
  (set plants)

In the late spring plant caraway and fennel and sesame (seeds or plants).

SUMMER:

You can plant angelica seedlings in early summer. Other summer-planted herbs are:

Lovage (seed, in late summer)
Sweet Basil (transplant seedlings when 4 inches high)
Thyme (seed, early summer)

Plant these herbs from the herb nursery in summer:

Ambrosia
Pot Marigold
May Apples
  (or pick wild)
Milkweed
  (or pick wild)
Mints
Stinging Nettle
  (pick wild)
Oregano

Chili Peppers
  (in the south)
Tabasco Peppers
  (in the south)
Purslane
  (pick in the wild)
Sage
Santolinas
Sweet Woodruff
Tarragon

FALL:

You can plant angelica seed in the fall. Other fall-planted herbs can be:

Lemon Balm
  (root division)
Calamus
  (set plants)
Catnip
  (seeds)

Spearmint
  (set plants)
Parsley
  (seed)
Rhubarb
  (root crowns)

118

Chamomile (seeds,
  or set plants)
Chervil
  (seeds)
Coriander
  (seeds)

Roses
  (set plants)
Winter Savory
  (root division)
Sweet Cicely
  (seeds)

Chapter 5.
Lawns:
Blades of Grass

I remember, once, when I was just finishing mowing Grandma Putt's lush green quarter-acre back lawn, I flopped down at her feet as she sat shelling peas under her favorite maple tree, "Great-Grandpa Coolidge."

"Grandma Putt, who invented the lawn mower?"

"A man named Hills," she said without even looking up.

Now, how my grandmother knew about Mr. Hills is a mystery to me. Years later, on a day when I had a little time on my hands, I spent several hours in my local library trying to find out about this Hills guy so I could give him the credit or the blame he deserves. But his name was not mentioned in any encyclopedia or gardening book that I could find. Then, when I was just about ready to give up, I checked in the World Almanac under inventions. Sure enough, right under "Mowers, lawn," was the notation, "Hills, USA 1868." In a way I'm sorry that Grandma Putt was right. I think that every work-weary husband and boy in America would rather blame the lawn mower on some evil Russian.

I've never been able to find a picture of Mr. Hills to see if he looked like a nice guy, but I'm sure that anyone who has ever spent a hot day pushing a hand mower can fashion a mental picture of him that is quite vivid!

Grandma Putt told me that Mr. Hills probably had a great deal of compassion for people. She said that before lawn mowers, people used to cut their grass with a scythe and that every year hundreds and thousands of men and boys would cut off their toes. She always thought that Mr. Hills invented the lawn mower as an act of mercy. She said that it was a tribute to the orneriness and perversity of humankind that we have since discovered a way to lop off toes and even fingers with power mowers.

When I insisted, she let me file-sharpen the old scythe hanging in the tool shed and try my hand at scything. But I couldn't seem to get the hang of it. Possibly because I was just a little bit afraid that I'd cut off my foot. Grandma said I shouldn't feel bad because mowing with a scythe is an art and requires lots of experience. She said that Great-Grandpa Coolidge had been able to scythe that whole quarter-acre lawn . . . "as clean as the lawn at Buckingham Palace in only twenty minutes."

After trying my luck with the dangerous-looking tool, I concluded that Great-Grandpa Coolidge must have been quite a man. Then, I willingly set about sharpening and oiling the noisy old lawn mower.

Incidentally, a few years ago, I visited England, and, one afternoon, I happened to see the gardeners at Buckingham Palace actually scything the lawn with a great deal of skill and dexterity. The tour guide told my wife and me that Buckingham Palace has one of the few great lawns in the world where the gardeners still use scythes instead of mowers!

Another thing I noticed about the lawn at Buckingham Palace, was that a big part of it was not grass, but chamomile. Grandma Putt shared that same kind of a lawn with royalty! She had lots of chamomile mingled in with her grass. She said that chamomile makes a fine lawn because it is so easy to take care of and cuts so evenly. She said that chamomile lawns were popular three- and four-hundred years back for games like croquet and lawn bowling. She told me that Great-Grandpa Coolidge had been very fond of lawn bowling and that he told her that the famous English Admiral, Sir Francis Drake, had played a historic game of bowls on a chamomile lawn the day before he went out and defeated the Spanish Armada!

Grandma Putt said that I must have been a throwback to my Indian ancestors the way I objected to mowing the lawn. She said that the Indians weren't even able to grow lawn because the native grasses east of the Mississippi weren't suitable for pasture lands. Lawns, she said, come to us from England and Europe. But the English developed the best ones because of the mild climate and the great amount of rainfall. She said that nobody but croquet players and lawn bowlers ever cut the grass. In fact, it was very fashionable to let it grow long.

The first lawns were an imitation of the open meadows and they were brought inside the medieval walled gardens because it was too dangerous for law-abiding citizens to go walking around the countryside in those days. When you think about how risky it is to walk alone through the parks of our modern cities, you begin to realize how little things have changed over the centuries. Anyway, back in medieval times, the lawns were often trampled, but uncut. It was the custom to sprinkle wild flowers here and there all over the lawn, and you couldn't cut the grass for fear of disturbing the flowers. I must admit, at age ten, I thought that was a splendid custom, a tradition, I believed, that should have been carried down to modern times.

Despite what we've all been led to believe, not all the damned fools are members of our generation or even a product of our times. Whoever it was who first cut or mowed the lawn is lost to human memory. But, someone came up with the idea and, like sheep, millions of us have followed his lead year after year. Speaking of sheep, Louis XVI of France was a great believer in the beauty of close-cropped lawns. For that purpose, he imported hundreds of sheep to graze on the grass at his fabulous new thirty-five million dollar residence at Versailles. The grass may have been great to look at, but it wasn't much to smell! Many of his courtiers complained about the odor of the palace lawns in their memoirs. Theodore Roosevelt must not have read those histories though, because he always had several sheep grazing the lawns of his Victorian mansion at Sagamore Hill in Oyster Bay, Long Island. Grandma Putt said it's better to have a boy cut your grass than a lamb. I guess we boys don't smell so bad after all.

The All-American Lawn

When people would ask, Grandma Putt would say that her beautiful green carpet of a lawn was "predominantly made up of Kentucky bluegrass." But, she always hastened to add, "It has a little of this and a little of that mixed in for good measure." She said that hers was a typical "all-American lawn."

After looking at thousands of lawns over many years, I have to agree with her. Most people's lawns do contain ". . . a little of this and a little of that." In most of the northern humid region of the United States, you will find these all-American lawns. They do have a predominant percentage of Kentucky bluegrass, but you'll find lots of other grasses and plants as well.

The grass that made Kentucky famous, Kentucky bluegrass, is the granddaddy of all the really good-looking lawn grasses in the United States. Most of those great-looking lawns we think we remember from our childhood were of Kentucky bluegrass. Interestingly enough, Kentucky bluegrass is not a single strain of grass, nor is it native to the "Bluegrass State." It is as old as Ancient Greece, and migrated to Western Europe and England during the Middle Ages, where it became known as "English grass." Bluegrass is made up of thousands of variations of the original strain that was imported from England in Colonial times. No one knows exactly how, but it beat Daniel Boone and the settlers to Kentucky and the Ohio Valley. For more than two hundred years it has been the basic seed or sod for most of the northern lawns in this country. Traditionally, Kentucky bluegrass grows best from the Atlantic seaboard west to Kansas. And, from the Canadian border south to Kentucky. With careful attention, Kentucky-bluegrass lawns have also been grown successfully further west and south.

It's easy to rhapsodize about this grass because of its tendency to grow very dense and erect, and because of its beautiful dark-green color. It grows best in the spring and fall. Unfortunately, the grass does not do well in the heat of the late summer months. During these hot months it goes into its dormant stage, so it is usually mixed with other grasses or legumes that thrive in the sun and heat. Some "pals" of Kentucky bluegrass who are willing to take up the summer slack, include the fine-leaf fescues, Meyer's zoysia in the south, or, in the north, one of the twentieth-century adaptations of Kentucky bluegrass. These are: merion, arboretum, Canada, delta, Newport, park, and Troy. The most traditional companion for Kentucky bluegrass sold in mixtures used to be a Eurasion clover called white Dutch clover.

Grandma Putt's lawn was planted before the development of the new variations or adaptations of Kentucky bluegrass. Even before the commercial availability of other good summer grasses like the fescues and the zoysias. In her day, clover was the "summer savior" of most green lawns. By July, the Kentucky bluegrass would begin to give in to diseases like mildew or to weeds like crabgrass. As the grass became dormant, the white Dutch clover would take over and keep the lawn green.

When Grandma first put in her lawn, clover was essential. Now, it is almost completely unknown in most grass seed mixtures. When clover does turn up in a lawn nowadays, it's usually treated like a weed. Lots of home gardeners know how persistent it can be if it has a mind to stay at your place.

One of the reasons clover has lost its appeal is that it stains clothing and becomes very slippery when even slightly wet. These two inherent problems have made it very unpopular with mothers, coaches, and playground superintendents. All of them are concerned about our kids playing on a clover lawn.

Grandma Putt never wanted to get rid of the clover in her lawn. To her, it was both beautiful and essential. She complained whenever winter lasted into April saying, ". . . it will kill off this year's clover." She approved of clover because it would "fight off the chinch bugs better than anything else in the lawn."

If you have clover in your lawn, I suggest you think twice before you decide to kill it off. If you don't intend to roll around in it, it's just as pretty as grass and makes a fine companion for your bluegrass.

If you don't want to "leave the clover where it's at," or depend on having "a harsh winter that stays through spring," you can eliminate clover with 2,4,5 TP. Once again, *follow the directions carefully!*

Preparing the Lawn for Mowing

On the late afternoon or evening of the day before I was supposed to do my duty with the lawn mower, Grandma would hand me a big bowl, a table knife, and an old pair of scissors. Then, together, we would go out and ". . . prepare the lawn for mowing."

We'd sit or kneel in the grass and start to work digging out dandelion greens and weeds. Grandma would save the dandelion greens for stewing or for soups and salads. If there were fresh dandelion flowers, she'd have me pick enough of them so she could have a nosegay or two—and for her yearly batch of dandelion wine.

She would cut a few chamomile flowers too. Later, after they dried, they would be suitable for making the chamomile tea which she set great store by. She believed that chamomile tea was the best remedy for stomach cramps and for the intestinal flu. My wife Ilene and I still give it to our kids for those troubles and I believe it works as well as any store-bought patent medicine.

My Grandma Putt had considerable knowledge of Indian herb medicines. She would find a good many of these medicinal herbs right in her yard. Among these were some of the common weeds we do battle against every year. Grandma said that it isn't right to hate weeds. "They're just plants who happen to be living in the wrong place." Chickweed, she often made into a poultice. Plantain she brewed into a wicked-tasting medicine that was supposed to be good for headaches. I secretly believed that it earned that reputation because it made you feel so sick to your stomach that you tended to forget about your headache! Applied to the skin, plantain could heal cuts and bruises. I was always willing to try her "Indian medicine" so I could show off and tell my pals about it. She said that the Kiowas used plantain leaves in their corn salads. I don't recall that she ever did, but if so, I'm sure I ate it with relish!

In those days, I had a small boy's curious appetite. I remember, once, I ate some grass. I figured that if the cows and horses and sheep liked it so much it must be good. Needless to say, I was a pretty sick fellow! Grandma laughed when I told her. She said I should have skipped the grass and tried the clover. Indians, she told me, were very partial to clover, especially when it was young and tender. After my experience with grass, I decided to skip the clover.

Every once in a while, when we were weeding the lawn, she or I would find a four-leaf clover. Usually, I got to keep it for good luck. Other times, she'd put it between the pages of her Bible to dry. She said it was all right to "believe in luck" as long as you put your trust in God.

Digging out weeds with a table knife is a terribly tedious job. But Grandma believed there was great value in "getting close to the earth" and "touching" it. She said that was really the most important reason for becoming a farmer or having a garden.

Usually, we would use the time to give each other accounts of what happened during the day. Or, if I was lucky, Grandma would tell me an Indian story.

The Indians had a great love of nature and the mysteries of the Great Spirit. Their stories reflect this reverence for Life. Some of their legends bear a striking resemblance to our own fairy tales. She told one story about an Indian boy and a magic seed that was very similar to "Jack and the Beanstalk."

In case you are wondering, there was plenty of crabgrass, plantain, chickweed, and horse grass in those days too. I had to dig them out with the table knife, especially in those months before the crabgrass went to seed (July and August). As you probably know, crabgrass grows low enough to escape the mower blades so hand digging is still the best way to remove it. It's not all that bad a way if you have youngsters and can make a game out of who digs out the most weeds. If there is too much to dig out, raise up the crabgrass so the mower can catch some of it. While mowing isn't the most effective method of fighting crabgrass, it will limit its ability to make seed. You will have to let the good grass around the crabgrass grow slightly taller than normal in order to keep the crabgrass in shade. It needs lots of direct sunlight in order to germinate and flourish. So, it can be "shaded" out of existence.

A good time-honored method for ridding your lawn of pesky weeds, is to apply a continuous program of what Grandma Putt and I call "good cultural practices." That is, dethatch your lawn properly and see that it is shampooed, aerated, fed well, and mowed often. Then, if all that fails, you might want to try a more "modern" method of removing weeds.

Use a preemergence treatment on grassy weeds like crabgrass, goose grass, horse grass, and chickweed. This should be applied while the seed is dormant, before it can germinate or sprout in the spring. It begins to work just as the seed begins to germinate.

As I will be continually pointing out in this book, very often the so-called "new" methods are really "old-fashioned" methods that had been forgotten and then are "rediscovered" by scientists. A case in point is the application of these "new" preemergent weed killers. They are based on one of the oldest techniques ever employed in the lawn grower's war against crabgrass. The idea is to apply the treatment just prior to germination, so it will attack the weed seed just as it germinates. In the old days, these preemergents were dangerous to earthworms and, therefore, to birds. Now, producers have eliminated the arsenate compounds previously used. The new preemergent weed killers are nontoxic to animals and can be utilized with perfect safety. But, remember this important rule for using any weed killer, fungicide, or pest-control treatment ... *be careful and follow the directions on the package.* If you do this with the preemergent weed killers, you should be able to get rid of crabgrass once and for all.

For the dicot (dicotyledon) or broad-leafed weeds, like chickweed, clover, plantain, and dandelion, you can use 2-4 D, a growth stimulator hormone that makes the plants grow themselves to an early old age. The hormone is usually combined with Banvel, a herbicide, and really knocks these weeds off in a hurry.

I want to make one point here before I go on. Grandma Putt would have been one of the first to use modern medicines like the preemergence weed killers and growth stimulators, if her cultural practices couldn't get the job done. She believed in using every practical means available to get the gardening results she desired. But she also believed in putting in an extra dose of good common sense whenever she set out to kill a troublesome pest, lest she cause herself some harm. She said many times that, "One year's weed is many years' seed." I think with all the shouting about weed killers today, by those for and those against, not enough people on either side are including Grandma Putt's prescription for common sense. Weed killers are fine, if you just pay attention to the directions on the package and use them properly. Remember, you wouldn't drink a gallon of Aureomycin to get rid of a common cold. The same idea holds true for weed killers. *Use your head and follow directions.*

How and When to Mow a Well-Established All-American Lawn

It was in that long-ago summer that I first learned there are right and wrong ways to mow the lawn. Here are a few simple instructions Grandma Putt taught me.

First of all, don't take cutting the grass for granted. It is very important that you cut at the right time and in the right way. If you don't know when to cut and how to cut, you will defeat your purpose which is to have a fine beautiful green lawn.

One reason we mow the lawn is to stimulate branching and root growth. Another is to keep the blades standing tall and straight. Another reason is to assure a good green color. When grass blades are cut off at the top, the chlorophyll is rushed up the blade to seal off the cut.

How would you like your dentist to pull a tooth without giving you gas or preparing you for the shock? Well this is what happens when you cut grass during the heat of the day. When grass is cut, it is exposed to elements it has thus far been protected from, heat and surface winds. The tunnels to the roots are also briefly exposed to these elements. I suggest you mow your lawn in the evening when the winds have subsided and the sun has settled low. It is the best and most comfortable time for both you and your grass. Grass should be cut when it is dry. Cut it in the evening and water the next morning. Mowing when the grass is too wet can cause the mower to build up with wet cuttings and then it will have a tendency to tear the blades instead of cutting them cleanly. Pulling and tearing weakens the grass blades and may dislodge the roots.

Keeping your grass at the proper height will improve its quality and density. Kentucky bluegrass will be greenest and healthiest between 1½ to 2 inches. If you have a crabgrass problem you may have to keep your bluegrass at two inches during the hot summer months. Merion should be cut somewhat shorter than most other bluegrass varieties. Keep merion at one inch.

How Often?

If you have a bluegrass lawn, you should cut it every two to three days. Of course the frequency with which you cut is really determined by how fast the grass is growing. During the spring period of heavy growth, cut often. As the season progresses, and you and the grass grow more tired, cut less often. Other grasses require different frequencies. Rye grasses and fescues should be cut twice a week. Bent grass every other day. And although I may be in a minority, I have found that dichondra thrives when it is cut as often as once a week.

If you are cutting your grass short, don't let it get long again before you mow it again. The smaller the portion of leaf surface you remove, the less of a shock it will be to your turf.

Most grass doesn't do well with a brush cut and don't think you can skip "next time" by cutting your lawn extra short this time. All you are doing is hurting the grass's ability to maintain itself at proper density. Too many close shaves like that and you will begin to see your fine-quality lawn thin out. Pretty soon, it won't be able to adjust to the day-to-day problems like overwatering, soil compaction, disease, and insects.

Of course there are exceptions to every rule. The exceptions to the No-Close-Shave Rule are: Bermuda grass, carpet grass, and centipede grass. These can be cut at a half inch or even slightly shorter. All these grasses should be cut with a reel-type mower.

Be prepared to change the height adjustment on your mower a couple of times during the growing season. Too many people set it and leave it. Remember, during the heavy growing season you can cut closer and more often; but in the middle of summer raise the height of the cut to the maximum noted on your grass charts.

How to Mow

In my first book, *Plants Are Like People,* I explained the mowing method approved by most turf experts. I will restate it here as simply as possible and throw in some advice from Grandma Putt.

Pick a reel or rotary-type mower, whichever suits you best. Decide if you want a mower that's powered or self-propelled. Grandma had an old riding reel mower but she preferred the self-propelled hand mower. She said she wanted to be able to smell the grass after it was cut. She pushed her old mower when she was well up into her seventies. I have to admit, the smell of fresh-cut grass is one of the great sensual pleasures; it can transport me, almost instantly, back to those wonderful days of my childhood.

Set your mower for the desired height.

See to it that the blades are well sharpened. If yours is an old machine, it should be sharpened at the beginning and the end of the growing season. Other times, you can take a flat stone to a reel-type mower's blades. It's a good idea to buy a new blade for your rotary mower every year. But don't throw the old one away. Have it sharpened and then alternate with the new blade every month. I don't want to get into the argument over which kind of mower is best. But it's only fair to warn you that eighty percent of all the accidents with power lawn mowers involve rotary mowers. Be careful. Make sure it's completely turned off before you touch the blade. I know that sounds pretty obvious, but *obviously* lots of people need to be reminded just like when Grandma told me not to cut off my toes with the scythe.

Grandma said that grass is like people in that it doesn't like to be constantly rubbed the wrong way. She said that once you run your mower around the exterior edge of your lawn, you can go ahead and be as creative as you want. At age ten,

I was fond of curved lines and diagonals, but sometimes I'd make straight rows lengthwise or widthwise just to vary the mowing pattern. And, that's the real secret of proper mowing. *Vary the pattern each time you mow.* Grass should be mowed from several directions, especially during the growing season. This insures that the grass blades never are allowed to grow in just one direction.

When you come back from the opposite direction of a previous cut, make sure your mower overlaps at least halfway. This makes sure that you don't miss grass that was rolled flat by the mower wheels.

Don't allow your grass clippings to fall back into the mown lawn. Save them. As you will find out later, these clippings helped to make the compost that was the key to Grandma's successful garden.

You should begin mowing when the grass, in the spring, reaches a height of two inches. And, mow well into winter . . . as long as you can continue unhampered by snow or a soggy lawn.

The New Grasses

I won't dwell overlong on the increasing popularity of new lawn grasses because they may not have a legitimate place in a book about old-fashioned gardening. However, the past few decades have brought some dramatic changes in the development and improvement of grasses. We can all thank those "delinquent gardeners" who will use any excuse to run off and play golf. Yes, the tremendous growth of that sport since WW II has created an enormous pool of money in an effort to find and develop new grass strains. The greenskeepers are looking for strains that will flourish under every climatic condition in this country. In the north, golfers want to play as soon as the snow begins to melt. In the south and south-west, they keep swinging away right through the rainy winter season. Small wonder that the greenskeepers' association has financed a great part of the USDA's quest for hardy and easy to manage new turf strains. Although Grandma Putt never wielded a driver or a nine iron, I know she would have been the first to applaud the greenskeepers and the USDA for an important leap forward in lawn management. It wouldn't be right to disregard these new grasses—most of them variations of that old standby, Kentucky bluegrass. In the following short list I have attempted to capsulize the good and bad qualities of some of these new grasses. It does take quite a long time to assess their value to the home gardener so be careful when someone tries to sell you an unproven new "wonder grass." All of these listed below, are available com-mercially to the home gardener in most garden centers.

How New Bluegrass Strains Are Discovered

In every all-American lawn, you might be able to find up to a thousand variations of the original strain of Kentucky bluegrass that was first sown there. Since this grass is a hardy perennial, every so often a phenomenon known to scientists as a spontaneous mutation will occur, producing a brand-new adaptation of the original strain.

These variations of the common Kentucky-bluegrass strain may have particular characteristics which we lawn gardeners find appealing. For instance, a new variety may be stronger and tougher and be able to withstand a great deal of traffic and wear. Another may be a more brilliant green color and have the ability to keep this brilliance through the hot summer months or in periods of drought.

Remember though, that selective breeding for specific characteristics often creates strains that have inherent weaknesses. An analogy can be made with the inbreeding of animals like racehorses and pedigreed dogs. These animals are beautiful and perform well in specific aspects, but at the same time they can be very neurotic and high-strung. They are often more susceptible to disease and injury than mixed or mongrel breeds.

According to the United States Golf Association, there are over 1,100 native and introduced grasses in this country. Probably 25 or less have any real value to the home gardener. You will have to make your selection based on local soil conditions, climatic considerations, and the use you will expect to be getting from your turf. Following are the most commonly used bluegrass variations:

MERION

Merion was one of the first and best variations of Kentucky bluegrass. It was developed by the USDA's experimental Arlington Farms in the early 1930s. All the merion seed we are using today came from a single patch of grass sent to the Department of Agriculture by the greenskeeper at the Merion Country Club in Ardmore, Pennsylvania. This grass was discovered growing well and of a fine deep green color in a period of extreme drought when the surrounding bluegrass had wilted and burned out. The new merion Kentucky bluegrass was quickly developed commercially and is now the most important strain in fine grass seed mixtures sold to homeowners of the northern humid region.

Merion does however take a long time to germinate and is susceptible to rust. This can be overcome by adequate feeding of a high nitrogen fertilizer. Merion does best when kept cut at about one inch long. Rust normally attacks the tips of the leaves. If you mow at least once a week, you'll be safe and not sorry.

ARBORETUM

Arboretum was developed by the Missouri Botanical Gardens from selections of grasses taken from old lawns all over that state. It is a taller-growing adaptation of Kentucky bluegrass. It may do somewhat better south of the Ohio River, but it will take years of testing to prove this out. I'd say stick with Kentucky bluegrass and forget arboretum.

CANADIAN

I almost decided not to mention this variation because of its tendency to become stemmy. It can grow well if mixed with other finer grasses. It is most suitable where the winters are long and hard. It will grow well in the shade and where the soil is not very fertile. If you live far north of Seattle, you might want to give it a try.

DELTA

This variation was developed in Ottawa, Canada. Its best characteristic is that it is very quick to germinate (takes less than a week). It is a fast, vigorous, and dense grower. Used alone, it can be better than merion or common Kentucky bluegrass the first growing season. After that, it readapts the dominant characteristics of common Kentucky bluegrass. It is very good for beating out weeds because it quickly sets such a dense turf. However, like most thoroughbreds, delta has a built-in weakness. It has a very high susceptibility to the leaf spot fungus and is not recommended for use in areas where this disease is prevalent. You will find delta in many grass-seed mixtures with merion. They make good partners on your lawn.

I recommend that you use straight merion and just make it germinate more quickly by fooling it in the refrigerator. I'll explain how to do that later in this chapter.

NEWPORT

Developed in Pullham, Washington, this variation grows lower and more vigorously than most Kentucky bluegrass. It is more rust resistant than other strains, but after the first year, it may thin out. This is another grass I advise you to by-pass.

PARK

Park was selected at the Minnesota Agricultural Experiment Station. Most experts agree that this is just another bluegrass strain with no marked superiority over merion or delta.

TROY

Since I happen to live in Troy, Michigan, and can remember reading about the heroic fields of Troy in Homer's *Odyssey,* I was hoping for something exceptional from this variation. It was selected from imports from Turkey that were developed in Montana. Troy develops a coarse open turn even when well-fertilized, watered, and watched over. It isn't meant for your lawn.

WINDSOR

This is a name you will find on the package of many seed mixtures in the East and Middle West. Actually it is not much different from delta or merion. If necessary, you can substitute it for the former.

SHADE GRASSES

Sunlight is something every type of grass needs to carry on photosynthesis. All grasses need at least a little sun in order to green up. However, some grasses have proven better than others in shady areas. If part of your lawn lies in the shade most of the day, and no proper amount of tree trimming corrects the problem, you might want to try one of the grasses mentioned in this section. I won't guarantee any of them as best, they each have some shade tolerance that makes them worth a try.

Rough-stalked meadow grass. This grass burns out in heavy direct sunlight. You will find it in most shade-grass mixtures. If you use it, keep this area of your lawn well fed with a high nitrogen fertilizer and very well watered. This grass likes very moist soil.

Rye grasses. Rye-grass varieties are also sold as shade grass. I'm not too fond of these grasses in other areas. You can try sowing a variety of ryes under trees. Add a small amount of new seed every couple of weeks.

Annual bluegrass. This is a very controversial grass. Not too long ago, suppliers were saying this was a new wonder grass. Now it has fallen into disrepute and is often considered a weed by good turf men. One reason for criticizing it is that annual bluegrass has a tendency to become very spotty. You can overcome this if you feed it with a very high nitrogen-fixing fertilizer. This grass has a very bright and attractive green color. It grows very early in the spring and it seems to thrive where there is a very small amount of sunlight. In the light of recent reports on this grass I would try it in your hard-to-cover shady spots. It is probably better for your lawn than rough-stalked meadow grass or rye.

The fescues. Compared to all others, the fine-leafed fescues make the most sense for planting in the shady areas of your lawn. These are truly fine grasses and they are good companions for Kentucky bluegrass and its variations. In addition to their abilities or characteristics as good shade grasses, fescues do not need all the feeding and watering needed to maintain other shade grasses. Among the fine-leafed fescues you will find: red fescue, Illahee, Old Penn State, Pennlawn, Ranier, Trinity, and some newer experimental strains. My preference is the Pennlawn variety. It has proven to be the most disease resistant. Check with your local garden experts for advice on the best shade fescue for your local growing conditions.

The bents. I will give you more information on the bent grasses later in this chapter. They do make very good shade grasses, especially Highland bents and velvet bents. Try them if you can afford the time and the money. They are like fine ladies and take a lot of attention and care.

Grass Seed Mixtures

Most grass seed you get these days is sold in prepackaged mixtures. I am not entirely against mixtures. Most of my best pets have been mongrel pups, and I really believe the different kinds of grass which come from different parts of the country love to congregate together and tell each other the news of the day. No lawn that I have ever seen contains just one kind of grass. That is almost as unworkable and ridiculous as human segregation in our large cities. In grasses, some of the different strains can help the predominant strain in fighting off disease and solving different problems.

If Grandma Putt were here today, I'm sure she would react to the packaged grass-seed mixes like the lady in that TV commercial of a few years ago. She'd say, "I'd rather do it myself!" That's right, there's nothing to prevent you from making your own superior grass-seed mixture. Here's how to do it.

First, decide what strain of grass you want to be predominant in your lawn. You can do this by consulting your area's Agricultural Experiment Station or one of the experts at a nearby "Ag" college. If there are none of these in the area, ask your neighbors or a reputable seed supplier what grass thrives best in your locality. In the case of a neighbor, I suggest you check out his lawn before you ask his advice. It's been estimated that one in eight home owners has planted the wrong grass for his lawn.

Once you know which grass is best, use the highest percentage possible of that seed.

SELECTING SEED

Remember, there are different grades of seed. Usually the best is the most expensive. But that isn't always a safe and sure rule, so *read the label!* The USDA requires that packaged seed in this country clearly state on the package certain information regarding purity, germination, other grasses, and weed or inert matter.

For instance, if the seed you are buying is Kentucky bluegrass, you will want to know several things. How much pure Kentucky bluegrass is in this package of seed? Make sure that the highest possible percentage is present—true to its name on the package. How long will it take this seed to germinate and how much of it will germinate? You naturally want as large a percentage as possible to germinate. How much of the bluegrass seed is really other grasses? How much of it is weeds or inert matter? All this should be stated on the package.

YOUR OWN PRIVATE BLEND
Now that you have made your seed selections based on purity, good germination percentage, etc., you can begin to mix them together. For most lawns, I suggest either this traditional mixture:

> 40% Kentucky bluegrass
> 25% delta or Windsor bluegrass
> 35% creeping red fescue

Or, try this mixture of newer strains:

> 50% merion
> 25% Pennlawn creeping fescue
> 25% delta or Windsor Kentucky bluegrass

If you are the antsy type who must have quick cover, you can add 5-10 percent Red Top to either mixture subtracting from the lesser strains and leaving the Kentucky bluegrass (Mix 1) or the merion (Mix 2) intact.

PREPACKAGED GRASS-SEED MIXTURES
If a prepackaged mixture is the only seed available, and you don't want to contact other sources, go ahead. But *be careful! Read the labels!* Check for purity, germination and other percentages in these packages too. Look out for any but a minimal percentage of rye grasses. If there is any percentage of Kentucky 31, Alta Fescue or Timothy, avoid the mixture. These last three are absolutely no good for your

lawn unless it stretches for several acres. Even then keep these away from the grass closest to your house. In general, the best mixtures will have similarities to the percentages in the ones I suggested you mix for yourself. These mixes are good for most lawns in the northern humid region. You can substitute other strains which will grow better in your area if you live in the South or the West. The theory that a mixture with many varieties in one package will do better year round is ridiculous. Instead, choose a mixture with one predominant strain.

Other Kinds of Lawns

Grandma Putt never lived west or south of Oklahoma, so her experience with growing lawns in the Deep South and Far West was limited. Here are some of the most common grasses used in those areas.

The South

St. Augustine grass is a creeping perennial. It is a runner type of grass whose runners produce short leafy branches. It grows very well in northern and mid-Florida where the soils are moist and spongy. This grass is good for a play yard because it can really take a beating. It is one of the exceptions to the "no close shaves" rule. It develops a turf that is often very coarse, but is still one of the most widely used grasses in the South. If the soil is not fertile and you intend to use this grass, I suggest you feed it heavily with a high-nitrogen fertilizer. This grass is propagated by sprigs and plugs.

Bermuda grass makes a fine to fair lawn grass in the hot and warm parts of the United States. It used to be propagated by sprig planting, but now seed is commercially available. It can make a beautiful lawn if you commit your time and energies to caring for it. It does have a tendency toward stemminess. In order to prevent this from happening, you will have to keep it moderately watered, top dressed, and well brushed. Some improved varieties have been developed in recent years. These are Bayshore, Everglades I, Ormond, Sunturf, Texturf IF, Texturf 10, Tifgreen, Tiflawn, Tifway, U3, and Uganda. With all the bad publicity the country of Uganda has been getting lately, you may not be attracted to this variation. It really was developed in Cairo, Egypt, and produces a low growing and fine textured turf that is tolerant to cold weather. Much testing is still necessary before it becomes widely available. The U-3 adaptation is, like common Bermuda grass, becoming available in seed form and this is another Bermuda strain that can be grown successfully farther north and west. It is also cold tolerant. One of the problems with Bermuda grass is that it turns purple with the advent of cold weather. Having a purple lawn can make you the talk of the neighborhood! If you live in the South, I suggest you contact your regional Agricultural Experiment Station for information as to the suitability of these Bermuda grass variations.

The zoysias. If you don't like to mow the grass, you'll love the slow growing zoysias. They grow well in sun and shade and can take more traffic than most grasses. Known as Japanese lawn grass, zoysias were first brought to our shores from Siberia and Korea. Zoysia is highly weed-resistant and has been known to crowd out crabgrass. It is becoming more and more common in northern states although best suited to

146

the South. You can grow the newer Meyer and Emerald zoysias from seed, but all the zoysia varieties are most commonly sprig planted. Meyer's zoysia looks so much like merion that I once considered it for my own lawn here in Michigan. But I discarded the idea because the grass turns brown in the winter and stays that way until late, late spring. Other than this inability to cope with sub-zero temperatures, Meyer's zoysia is a very fine grass which makes a near-perfect lawn.

There are some other grasses which do well in the hot, humid southland. They are centipede and carpet grasses. Centipede, introduced from China, is a low-growing grass that is what we professionals call a creeper. It produces a very easy-to-care-for lawn that can look quite nice. It's a coarse-looking foliage, but has done well in poor soils where other grasses have failed. I believe it is more worth your time to build up the soils in your yard than to resort to centipede grass. However, if you have lots of acreage and don't want to become a slave to your lawn, this grass will work all right the farther away from the house that you get. It is certainly better than St. Augustine or carpet grass.

Carpet grass can be found almost everywhere in the warm coastal states off the Atlantic coast. It produces a very coarse and wiry grass and the seed is easily available and very cheap. It grows very well in shady areas, but needs very fertile soil and lots of feeding with a high-nitrogen-producing fertilizer. I'm not a big fan of this grass, and if you ever try pushing a lawn mower against it, you'll find out one of the reasons why. If you live in the South use a zoysia or Bermuda grass first. I'd even use St. Augustine or buffalo grass before this grass.

The West

Selecting a proper grass for the western part of the United States can be a pretty tricky job, because of the tremendous variations of climate and altitude.

As a general rule, all the cool-season grasses do well in all the West except southern California and the southwestern states. If you have the time, money, and energy you can even grow cool-season grasses in these southwestern areas. Otherwise, you will want to use one of the subtropical grasses mentioned earlier for the hot, humid, southern zone. In that case you will probably want to use common Bermuda grass or U3 Bermuda. If you don't mind the propensity of the zoysias to get brown in the winter, you can use Meyer's zoysia or Japanese lawn grass (zoysia). These grasses both do a good job fighting off dicot-type weeds.

Dichondra

During a period in the 1960s I thought there might not be any grass lawns left in Southern California and in parts of Arizona and Nevada. The reason was a tremendous boom in the sale and planting of dichondra. Dichondra is not a grass. It is a legumous groundcover which grows remarkably well in the western and southwestern climate. Once it gets a good start, it thrives in sun or shade and makes an ideal low-growing substitute for grass.

In the west-central region, the fine-leafed fescues, western crested wheatgrass, Kentucky bluegrass or merion do well. In nonirrigated areas you may have to resort to Vereening Bermuda grass or Texturf or if worst comes to worst, buffalo or St. Augustine grass.

Not all grasses should be planted, or grow best, from seed. Here is a chart showing the most commonly used sprig, stolon, or sod planted varieties. . . .

Seed Chart

COMMON LAWN GRASS SEEDS	RATE 1000 FEET	TONE OF GREEN	LOCATION AND USE
KENTUCKY BLUEGRASS (*Poa pratensis*)	2 lbs.	Medium	Sunny, will tolerate slight shade. Medium texture.
MERION BLUEGRASS (*Poa pratensis*)	1 lb.	Dark	Sunny, will tolerate slight shade. Medium texture.
ROUGH STALK MEADOW (*Poa trivialis*)	2 lbs.	Light	Wet, shade. Shiny leaf.
CHEWINGS FESCUE (*Festuca rubra*, var. *fallax,*	3 lbs.	Medium	Dry, shade and poor sandy soil. Fine texture.
CREEPING RED FESCUE (*Festuca rubra*)	3 lbs.	Medium	Sandy soil. Fine texture.
HIGHLAND BENT (*Agrostis tenuis*)	½–1 lb.	Dark	Sun and light shade. Fine texture.
TALL FESCUE (*Festuca elatior*)	6–10 lbs.	Light	Athletic fields, etc. Coarse, striated leaf.
ASTORIA BENT (*Agrostis tenuis*)	½–1 lb.	Bright	Sun and light shade. Fine texture.
SEASIDE CREEPING BENT (*Agrostis maratima*)	½–1 lb.	Meduim	Sun and light shade. Fine texture.

PENNCROSS CREEPING BENT *(Agrostis palustris)*	½—1 lb.	Dark	Sun and light shade. Fine texture.
REDTOP *(Agrostis alba)*	1—1½ lbs.	Medium	Used in mixtures. Medium texture.
ANNUAL RYE GRASS *(Lolium multiflorum)*	3—4 lbs.	Medium	Temporary lawns and in mixtures. Coarse texture.
PERENNIAL RYE GRASS	3—4 lbs.	Dark	Temporary lawns and in mixtures. Coarse, shiny leaf.

COMMON LAWN PLANTED PLUGS	RATE PER FOOT	TONE OF GREEN	LOCATION
BERMUDA	1 sprig	Medium	Sun and dry. Coarse texture.
ST. AUGUSTINE	1 plug	Medium	Sun and dry. Coarse texture.
ZOYSIA	1 plug	Medium	Sun and dry. Coarse texture.

Some Grasses to Avoid

Most of us want a lawn we can be proud of and, because of overeagerness, we often succumb to far-out claims about so-called "miracle grasses" or "quick-growing" varieties. Some of these are fair to good grasses which are just over-advertised. Others, are the worst things possible for your lawn. Remember, there is nothing wrong with looking a gift horse in the mouth. Here are the least-desirable grasses.

Annual bluegrass. This is a grass that germinates very early in the spring and looks terrific. It may someday become widely accepted, but most grass and turf experts will advise you to steer clear of it until it has been scientifically developed for use in this country. Past performance has shown annual bluegrass has a tendency to look good in early spring and then die out in spots during the heat of summer. I'm sure none of us wants a "spotty" lawn. If you want to use this grass, have an expert put in your lawn and guarantee it. Maybe with lots of care and a good feeding program, it will have no problems.

Kentucky 31. Lots of people are fooled by the word "Kentucky" in the name. This is a tall fescue not a bluegrass. This grass is plain lousy for lawns. It can be found in the cheapest and least reliable grass-seed mixtures. It produces a very coarse sod. Look out for it unless you have lots of pasture-land and cows with strong teeth. One good thing you can say about Kentucky 31 is that "It takes a licking and keeps on ticking." . . . It does make a tough hardy utility or service lawn. Just make sure it never gets near the grass you want to be proud of or show off to your neighbors.

Alta fescue. Like Kentucky 31, this is a broad-leafed fescue that produces deep-rooted ugly sod. Forget it!

Redtop. This is a relative to the bents, but it's about as similar to good grass as corn or bamboo (both of which, technically, are grasses). Redtop is a fast starter and for that reason is used in grass-seed mixtures to give you that "quick green cover" while you are waiting for your merion or bluegrass to germinate. Be leery, because in the end you may have trouble getting rid of it. Don't believe what some misinformed people tell you about these so-called "nurse grasses." They compete for the same ground and sunlight that your good grasses need. Redtop is better than rye, but both can crowd out rather than "nurse" the good grass.

Saving the Best 'Til Last: The Bentgrasses

To paraphrase a current beer commercial, "If you've got the time, we've got the *grass!*" I'm talking about the bentgrasses. First, let me warn you from experience that the care and upkeep, time and work it takes to grow a successful bentgrass lawn can really turn into a full-time job. However, if you don't mind becoming a "grass sitter," the final result can be so beautiful your lawn will become the talk of the neighborhood. Perhaps the smoothest, finest looking lawns, outside of Astro-turf, are produced with bentgrasses. Among these are: colonial bents, creeping bents and velvet bents.

Colonial bentgrass is widely used. It can be obtained as seed or sod in several varieties including: Astoria, Estacada, Highland, New Zealand colonial (Browntop), Oregon colonial, and Prince Edward Island. This grass does very well in the cool humid northeastern region. Colonial grows rapidly and for that reason requires lots of water and a good fertilizer program. It can take very close cutting with a 6 to 8 blade reel mower. Colonial is often found in mixtures with other bentgrasses.

Creeping bentgrass is so named because it spreads by creeping stems or stolons. These stolons quickly produce roots and new growth at almost every joint. Before long, this grass will form a dense turf and a lawn that looks almost too perfect to be true! Two varieties are commercially available in seed for planting. These are Seaside and Penncross. Of the two, I prefer the Penncross.

Among the common bentgrass varieties for vegetative planting available now are: Arlington, Berkshire, Cedar Rapids, Cocoos, Congressional, Dahlgreen, Great Bend, Metropolitan, Old Orchard, Pennlu, Shawnee, Springfield, Sleepy Holly, Toronto, and Washington. All of these can make great-looking lawns, so ask around your area's reputable garden experts and find out which varieties do best in your local climatic and soil conditions.

Bentgrass vegetative planting material can also be purchased in mixtures. The theory behind this is the same idea for grass-seed mixtures: that the strengths and growing season of one variety will make up for the deficiencies and limitations of the next variety. If all goes well, you should have a beautiful green lawn the year round. I'd think twice about all this because the theory can work in reverse and you'll have one variety weakening the next. Also, be careful that the different varieties produce grass that's similar in color, or your lawn will look patchy. One rule of thumb for all kinds of grass is for you to decide on a strain you want to be predominant in your lawn, then stick with your choice. Then, you will be able to minimize your lawn disease potential to the particular built-in weaknesses of that one variety. You'd be surprised how many varieties have completely different weaknesses. Obviously, lots more of these deficiencies can show up in a mix than in one strain.

Creeping bent needs constant attention, lots of moisture and a good feeding program. It should be mowed at a height of three-quarters to one inch. It is susceptible to fungus infection, but this can be minimized with a good feeding program lime applications, and preventive fungicides.

Velvet bents. If the rose is queen of the garden, this is the velvet cloak to spread before her feet. Velvet bent lawns look too good to be true. This grass does best when you have done your homework and provided extremely fertile soil and what my Grandma Putt used to call "sweet" soil. Sweet soil has a low acidity. You will probably have to add lime east of the Mississippi several times a year. I say several times for a good reason. Giving your lawn a big dose of lime can bring on the "stomachache." Grandma advised several small "doses" of lime over a long period of time rather than one big application at the beginning of the growing season. She said that grass, like people, can't take such a big shock to its digestive system. In a way, it's like giving someone a whole bottle of Alka-Seltzer to relieve a little stomach acid. Remember, lime is not a food, but it increases the availability of food elements in the soil, and lets them do their jobs. It also can reduce toxic elements in the soil and inhibits the ability of fungus to get a start. If you help your bentgrass lawn in this way, it will form a dense turf that will eliminate weeds and fungus.

When You Care Enough to Have the Very Best

A man named Hodges was known to one and all as the richest man in the county. He owned the grainery and the hardware in town and was one of the directors of the bank.

In the late 1930s, when everyone was just hoping that the Depression was ending, Mr. Hodges decided to set a good example for the sagging local economy by building a rather pretentious house on some acreage he owned just south of town, not far from Grandma's place.

A few years later, when I lived with Grandma, the Hodges house was not only a local showplace, it was a good spot for a young boy to make some spending money mowing the grass, keeping up the grounds, and doing other chores.

Mr. Hodges had a regular gardener named Matt Komperda who was a good friend of Grandma's. So, whenever there was extra work of this sort, I got the first call.

The reason I brought all this up is because, that summer, Mr. Hodges decided to put in a creeping bent front lawn. He was the only man in the area who could afford such an extravagance. Bentgrass as you probably know makes a very beautiful lawn, but it is very expensive to plant and keep in tip-top condition. Of course Old Man Hodges didn't have to do the work himself. He left that to Matt and me.

When Matt and I first began to work on Mr. Hodges' lawn, we had several important preliminary tasks. The first was to peel up the perfectly good Kentucky bluegrass sod and save it. In those days, that was a very tricky procedure which we accomplished with square-edged spades and butcher knives. Today, there are machines to do the work we had to do with hand tools.

After the sod was lifted, rolled up and stored under soaked burlap, we set about preparing the soil for planting the bentgrass stolons. First, we mixed some sand in with the seeded loam. A sandy loam is the perfect foundation for a bentgrass lawn.

Using a hand cultivator, we loosened all the soil, mixing in good old garden gypsum, fifty pounds to each thousand square feet. Also the same quantity of a low-nitrogen high-phosphate fertilizer.

Creeping bents are surface growers and need moisture even more than they need fertile soil. So, after all these ingredients were mixed with the loosened soil, we stopped building our seedbed and laid out an underground watering system. That turned out to be a two-day job because Matt insisted on hooking it up above-ground first to make sure we had designed a system that provided adequate coverage. This is a valuable technique to remember if and when you decide to put in such a system. It can take you twice the work and twice the time to re-dig the pipe trenches and reconnect it under ground level if you don't get the right coverage the first time.

An automatic underground water system can be an important plus for a fine bentgrass lawn. It is not absolutely necessary, but these lawns require a great deal of watering. It can become a very time-consuming daily chore to drag out the hose and sprinklers every time you need water. It's also surprising how much damage dragging watering equipment across a bent lawn can accomplish. For automatic watering and adequate coverage, consider installing one of these systems.

Back in the 1940s, we used black iron pipe for Mr. Hodges' system. These days, the new plastic pipes are much easier to work with and are much less expensive than galvanized or black iron.

Once we had finished installing the watering system, we proceeded to complete the seedbed. Matt said it was important to make the top surface very smooth. Otherwise, any little bump, depression, or ridge would show up in the completed lawn and then we'd have twice the work correcting our mistakes. It's always better to take that extra time in the first place to make sure things are right. As Grandma Putt used to say, "Only God was ever able to complete a garden in a matter of days, we regular folk might as well relax and enjoy the sunshine."

It's a good idea to use a roller for this final step in smoothing the seedbed. Be sure that it is no more than half full of water. Also, never roll when the soil is wet. You'll be causing compaction after all that work you did loosening and mixing.

The final texture of the top layer of the seedbed should be crumbly, not grainy. You can overdo the working and re-working of your soil.

Preparing the Seedbed for an Entirely New Lawn

Since the Hodges lawn had previously contained a fine stand of Kentucky bluegrass, preparing the seedbed for bent-grass plantings wasn't overly difficult. But if you are planning to install a new lawn, where none has ever been before, follow these steps carefully.

Step I. Use a roto-tiller, hand cultivator, disc and harrow, or spade and hoe to loosen the soil in your seedbed. This should be done from a half foot down to twelve inches, depending on the root-building qualities of the grass you will be seeding or planting.

Step II. Pick out any rocks or debris turned up by your tilling. Don't miss anything. Your grass will not grow well over rocks, roots or shingles.

Step III. Take care of weed roots or insect pests present in the soil. Check with a reliable chemical expert. You don't want to sterilize your soil permanently before planting grass.

Step IV. Now apply fifty pounds of Grand Prize Gypsum per 1,000 square feet of soil. Next, in snow country, add 100 pounds of peat moss per 1,000 square feet. In the Southwest and West, you can use old sawdust, leaf mold, or well-rotted steer manure in the same proportion. If you are planting bentgrass or dichondra, you may have to add sand. One-half bushel per 1,000 square feet will be sufficient. Sandy loam makes the best seedbed for those types of lawns.

Step V. Next, add fifty pounds of any garden food with a low-nitrogen high-phosphorus content: 4-12-4 or 5-10-5 are fine. You want a fat, even-growing crop of grass.

Step VI. Mix all these ingredients with your roto-tiller. If you don't have a large lawn area, you can use a hoe and rake but it's a tough, muscle-stretching job. Renting the roto-tiller is worth every cent you will have to spend.

Step VII. Level off this cultivated soil. (Don't overwork it and pulverize the soil completely.) Now, go over it once more and pick up any additional stones, root twigs, and large inert matter.

Step VIII. Now check the level of your new seed bed. Make sure it's up to the height you desire for your lawn. If you are laying sod, it should be approximately 3/4 of an inch below the finished lawn level. If it is not up to the height you require, you will have to lay additional topsoil.

BEWARE of any topsoil you have to purchase. Don't be fooled by "good black dirt." It may be subsoil treated with a sludge to look like black topsoil. Color isn't the criterion here. Remember all that raking and picking over that you had to do with your own top soil? Well, check this soil you are considering. If there are stones, twigs, etc., go ahead and buy it. It probably is topsoil.

If you are buying topsoil, you will want to move Step III to the next position in your routine because you can be almost certain that any introduced topsoil will bring your lawn lots of weed seed and insects.

Step IX. Work the soil up around the foundation of your garage, sidewalks, drives, flowerbeds and trees. This is to force runoff and proper drainage. The idea of a completely flat lawn is a mistaken one except for bentgrass which does need a flat seedbed. Most lawns require a slight pitch or slope to assure good drainage. Your lawn should slope away from your house at a grade of 10 or 12 inches every hundred feet. That will keep heavy rainfall out of your basement during heavy rainfalls and will still allow your grass to receive its maximum water requirements to its deepest roots.

Step X. Now smooth the remainder of your lawn. For this purpose you can use your "fertile" imagination to find some helpful tools. My favorite is an old bed spring which you can usually find somewhere at home or in a neighbor's basement. Tie a rope on the front of it as you would on a sled. Pull the spring in big, over-lapping circles, stopping only to fill in or shave off spots. A five-foot length of chain fence, a heavy window frame or an old section of a ladder will serve nicely for this same purpose.

Now you are ready to seed or sod.

Planting A Creeping Bent Lawn

Creeping bentgrass wasn't very commonplace in home lawns in the forties, at least not out near my Grandma Putt's. But it had been used for years as a perfect grass for the greens of golf courses. Matt and I had to obtain Mr. Hodges' bentgrass plantings from a golf course nearly forty miles away. The sod had already been run through a shredder, so the plantings were in sprig form.

If you are making your own stolon plantings from sod or nursery flats, you can separate the clumps of stems by hand. Tear off pieces about two inches long with a few leaves on each sprig. If you have a very large lawn, I would suggest you not do all this time-consuming work yourself. Instead, have the nursery where you purchase your vegetative material chop or shred the stolons for you. Sprig plantings are also sold in plastic bags, ready for planting.

Once you bring the shredded stolons home, be sure to use them as quickly as possible. They are easily damaged by lack of moisture, overhandling or overheating. In our case, we couldn't plant them right away so we spread them out to prevent overheating and rotting. Then we protected them from drying out with a covering of coarse burlap which we kept constantly saturated with water.

Proper vegetative planting of bentgrass and most southern grasses takes three basic forms: plug planting, sprig (stolon) planting, and laying sod.

Plug Planting

I have known people who grew up in some parts of the South who were surprised to find, after moving north, that there are ways other than "plugging" to plant grass. This system is used primarily for Bermuda grasses and dichondra.

Plugs are small chunks of grass which can be extracted from good turf, nursery flats, or sod with a tool called a plugger. If you are planting dichondra, ask for a dichondra transplanter. These tools take out a chunk that's a couple of inches long and three to four inches deep. If you haven't overworked your seedbed soil and made it too fine, you can use the same tool to cut out the holes where you intend to plant. The holes should be placed about a foot apart. Both the plugs and the seedbed should be presoaked so the roots will keep moist. I mean moist, not muddy. I've said this many times before, "grass can't swim." The plug should be placed in a hole and then pressed down firmly with the palm of your hand until level with the surface. Take the time to make sure you get them level with the surface or you will have a lumpy-looking lawn. You will need about ten rows of plugs for every 1,000 square feet of lawn. After planting, roll the entire area with an empty roller. Keep well watered.

Plugs are notoriously slow starters. It normally takes as long as two full years to get a good dense turf. Here are a couple of good tips. First, be sure to do your "plugging" during the most propitious planting time for the grass you are using. Spring and early summer are best for the southern and southwestern grasses like Bermudas, buffalo grass, carpet grass, centipede, St. Augustine and zoysias. Late summer or early fall are the best times for bentgrass.

Second tip: presoak the plugs in a very weak solution of water, a mild dishwashing liquid (biodegradable) and high-nitrogen fertilizer. Use this same solution on your planted lawn every other week all during the growing season.

Sprigging

This is the type of vegetative planting Matt and I used on Mr. Hodges' lawn. It is a method that was developed by greenskeepers. It's much less expensive than laying sod or plugging and seems to bring very fast reliable results. The sod is run through a simple shredding machine and the resulting stolonate sprigs are hand-broadcast over the presoaked seedbed. We used approximately three bushels of sprigs for each 1,000 square feet of lawn.

After the sprigs were down, we rolled the area with an empty roller and applied a half-inch layer of top dressing.

Top Dressing

After planting sprigs or sod, it's best to apply a thin layer of top dressing. This consists of a mixture of loose soil, sand, and peat moss. You may want to substitute a package of nonorganic top-dressing material, like perlite, or vermiculite. The idea is to dress the lawn surface with a material that holds moisture and is coarse enough to prevent compaction.

Sodding

Sodding is one of the few home-gardening jobs that offers immediate results and immediate success. Laying sod is an old English technique, one that British home gardeners have perfected into an art. Here, in the United States, sodding has been used as a vegetative planting technique for establishing new greens and tees on golf courses. With the boom in building after WW II, sodding became a quick way for developers to establish lawns for model homes, plants, and offices. The invention of new machinery for cutting and rolling sod encouraged growers to build up an enormous industry. While sodding is still an expensive lawn planting method for most homeowners, it has become more and more popular.

My advice is that if you can afford to lay sod for your lawn, have a professional do it. That way, you'll get a smooth-looking lawn without humps and bumps.

One problem with sodding is that nonprofessionals tend to take their new "instant lawn" for granted. As Grandma Putt used to say, "You've got to think perpendicular." What she meant was that you have to look at more than what's above the ground. You can't afford to forget or ignore what's going on under the ground. Plants are like people, sometimes beauty is only skin deep. Underneath the grass skin, you either have a vigorous, healthy organism or one that is unhealthy and functioning poorly. Sod has to develop a strong vigorous root system in order to be able to thrive and fight off lawn diseases and insect pests.

DOING IT YOURSELF

If you insist on laying your own sod, here are some tips.

1. When selecting sod, pick a good-quality grass that grows well with this planting method. Bentgrass, merion or Kentucky bluegrass are the top-quality sods for the northern part of the U.S. Zoysias, dichondra and some bents make good sod in the South and Southwest.

2. Thin sod does best. Contrary to what you might think, thin sod seems to work more quickly to establish good contact with a new loam bed. Select sod three-quarters of an inch thick.

3. When you are preparing your loam bed for sod, make it three-quarters of an inch lower grade than if seeding, plugging, or sprigging.

4. To figure how much sod you will need, multiply the length of your lawn area by the width, and then divide by nine.

5. If your sod must be kept somewhere before laying, store it grass-side up. Keep cool and dry.

6. Before you lay down your sod apply a layer of slow-working ureaform fertilizer to the top surface of your loam bed.

7. Lay sod the way a bricklayer lays brick, with the strip ends staggered. Make sure that there are no gaps between the ends. Peg the sod down to insure good contact with the loam bed. Apply a thin top dressing to the cracks between ends and joints. Roll with a half-filled roller.

8. Now follow a good feeding and watering program. Use the water, soap, and nitrogen solution described on page 60. Don't overwater. It's not as necessary to keep this as soaked as the top surface of a newly seeded lawn. You want those roots to get started looking for moisture and nutrients in the soil.

9. Give your new sod lawn a week to ten days to set before you mow. Frequent mowing will encourage the roots to begin growing. Don't let merion or bluegrass get much taller than an inch between mowings. Start cutting bentgrass at an inch, but after two or three cuttings lower your mower to one-half to three-quarters of an inch.

Seeding Your New Seedbed

Despite all the improved techniques in vegetative planting, old-fashioned seeding is still the safest and surest way to start an exceptional lawn.

WHEN TO SEED

When to seed is just as important as how to seed. With merion and Kentucky bluegrass, late summer and early fall are the best times to sow. Fall sowing gives your lawn a good start in a season when weeds are not competing with them. The list below will give you proper seeding times.

> Bermuda *spring*
> buffalo grass *spring*
> creeping bent *spring*
> perennial ryes *spring—fall*
> created wheatgrass *fall*
> Kentucky bluegrass *fall*
> red fescue *fall*
> redtop *fall*

HOW TO SEED

Seed can be sown by hand-broadcasting or mechanically. Figure out the amount of seed you will need. This can be done by checking the directions on the package. If you are making your own mixture from the percentages listed earlier, figure the amount you will need to sow based on requirements for the predominant strain you are using.

Grandma Putt taught me an interesting trick that you might want to try. Take the amount of seed you intend to use and divide it into four parts. This simple procedure will help remind you not to oversow in spots during one or two applications.

FOOLING THE GRASS

For those of you who have not read *Plants Are Like People,* here is another short-cut to help your grass get off to a good start. As I mentioned, most grass grows best from August 15th to September 20th. This is the time of the harvest moon. The evenings are cool and there is more moisture in the air. If you want your grass to germinate quickly, here's how to fool the seed into thinking it's the time to germinate. Add one cup of water with two table-spoons of tea. Best way is to have a nice cup of tea yourself and give your seed a cup or two. Give it two tablespoons of tea per pound of seed. Mix it well, place in a covered container and put it in the refrigerator for five days. Remove the seed from the refrigerator and spread it out on the garage or basement floor to allow for partial drying. Sweep the floor, do a good job to please the lady of the house. Be careful not to include any nails, broken glass, or grease. Now, you are ready to spread this combination of seed and dirt on your lawn. The grass has been tricked into going into a forced "winter" dormancy and is now ready to germinate. Grandma Putt was pretty crafty, getting me to do two jobs at the same time and thinking I was having fun!

I believe in hand broadcasting. This is the way I was taught. Check the wind with that first handful or with some paper. For your first approach, back across the property with your back to the wind and throw the seed in the direction you are coming from. Next go back and rebroadcast cross-wind. Next, crosswind in the other direction. For your last approach, go into the wind. Of course, you shouldn't be sowing on a windy day, but if the wind is blowing too strongly, rebroadcast with the wind as in your first approach. Roll your new lawn with an empty roller.

To Mulch or Not to Mulch?

Whether or not you will want to mulch your newly seeded lawn depends really on local wind problems and on your ability to water properly. I'm not much for mulching, especially the old idea of straw mulching. Straw can bring lots of weed seed. That's a pretty cruel blow after all the work you've done.

When watering, keep the newly seeded area moist at all times. Use a sprinkler or hose setting that is as close to a mist as possible. You don't want to wash any seed away. If you do wash some away, resow immediately.

Maintaining Your All-American Lawn

Grandma Putt used to say that taking care of your lawn over a period of years is like looking after the health of a close friend or relative. She said that we should take care of our lawns the way the ancient Chinese practiced medicine. The Chinese believed that you hired a doctor to keep you well. Then, if you got sick, you fired the doctor and got a new one. Obviously, your lawn isn't going to fire you if it gets sick. But if you follow the simple cultural practices and a good commonsense lawn-care program, you won't have to spend a lot of time and money tearing your lawn up and starting all over.

The Cultural Practices That Keep Your Lawn Well

If God provides the sunshine and you provide the program and the elbow-grease, there is no reason you can't have the best lawn in town. Here is a month-by-month program like the one I applied to caring for Grandma's lawn years ago.

JUNE

Early in the month, I gave the lawn its second light dethatching of the year. The thatch is an accumulation of old clippings and debris that had built up at the base of the grass stems over the year. Give your lawn a vigorous raking with a wire rake to get out this dandruff. After dethatching, I aerated the soil. In those days, I used the tines of an old pitchfork. Now, I use my golf spikes whenever I work on the lawn. Ilene won't let me use my good ones, so I've kept an old pair for lawn work. Of course you can rent or buy a power rake or aerating tool which punches holes and pulls out the dirt. Any one of these tools can work. Just let your grass breathe and it will really go to work for you.

On Grandma's wash days, I would empty the wash water over different areas of the grass. You can do the same thing much more easily and effectively. Use a mild dishwashing soap applied with a hose-end sprayer. This kind of shampoo application serves as a surfactant, getting rid of dirt and warding off insects and disease. It also gets rid of dirt on the grass blades and promotes normal feeding and photosynthesis.

Use one ounce of liquid soap per 10 gallons of water for each 1,500 square feet of lawn.

Edging around the sidewalks, trees, walls, and shrubs this early in the year will help keep your lawn in bounds and from drying out or shading out in these areas. Use gypsum under the shrubs and around the trees as a mulch.

I found some moss on the north side of our maple tree, "Great-Grandpa Coolidge." Grandma said this showed the area was getting poor drainage due to compaction. She had me aerate and apply some gypsum here too.

You should apply your monthly dose of fertilizer in June.

JULY

Grandma's advice is to let the lawn rest during July. This is its hardest working time. It uses up lots of energy growing, fighting the hot weather, and trying to ward off diseases. While the grass was doing all this work, she had me lay off any heavy maintenance. July lawn attention includes regular mowing, digging crabgrass and weeds. And, of course, paying extra-careful attention to watering.

AUGUST

The early part of August you should leave your grass alone. Grandma said it was too hot to pick on the lawn.

From August 15th on through, you can begin to overseed in bare spots. If you just moved in and the lawn is lousy, this is the time to start making friends with your soil and planting a brand new lawn. Sodding can be done now, or at almost any time of the year.

Water well, as soon as the soil beneath the surface dries out. This may be every day at the beginning of the month.

Watch out for insect and disease problems. August is bug month in most states. Apply the proper controls with the proper care. Chlordane will be your old standby. Fertilize with a high-nitrogen fertilizer.

SEPTEMBER

Early September it's still all right to plant grass by seed or sod. Later in the month, give the lawn its third yearly dethatching. Make this one gentle too. After dethatching, give the grass a shampoo.

OCTOBER

I applied gypsum to the lawn as a top dressing. This is

especially important for city lawns now because of salt damage from snow and ice-melting materials.

NOVEMBER

October or November is the last time to fertilize for the year. Use a low-nitrate, high-phosphate and potash fertilizer for this job. It will help insure the grass's survival over the cold winter months.

DECEMBER AND JANUARY

Now you can watch football being played on Astro-turf and forget your lawn. But after the Bowl games, begin to think about any major jobs you and your lawn will be sharing next year. This is the time to bring your tools into the garage or workshop and clean them and repair them. Surprise your hardware man by bringing your lawn mower in for a tuneup and sharpening now. It may not be any cheaper, but it will sure beat the spring rush. Late January or February is also the time to start buying any tools you'll be needing. Nothing is more frustrating than to do without the proper tools in April or May because they're sold out.

FEBRUARY

Pick up your lawnmower before he loses it in his stock-room. There's nothing wrong with seeding or feeding right on top of the snow during the first two or three months of the year. As a matter of fact it will give your lawn a good spring start and help it fight weeds later.

MARCH

If crabgrass was a problem, use a preemergent control for it now.

After the weather turned nice, I broom-raked the whole lawn area with a flexible bamboo lawn rake. It's all right to use a flexible steel or wire rake for this if you want to. Just be careful not to pull up any grass by the roots. The ground is usually still very damp from wintering. Do it as gently as you would like someone to scratch your scalp if you just woke up.

Your lawn needs feeding now to prepare it for the spring growth spurt. There's nothing wrong with changing lawn food from time to time. Just like humans, grass likes a varied diet.

APRIL

If you didn't seed in February or March, April is still all right. Do it early in the month. Don't seed and apply pre-emergent crabgrass killer at the same time. The weed control can prevent your grass seed from germinating.

April is the time for your first dethatching and aerating of the year. After dethatching, shampoo. Then mow the dried grass down to one inch and don't let April showers boost it past that height.

If April is a dry month, water every other day before 2 p.m. Make sure you saturate the soil to a depth of three inches. Grandma taught me to put a big tin can in the path of the sprinkler so I could check on this before moving to another part of the lawn.

MAY

This is dandelion month, so I feed the lawn with weed and feed treatments. These have improved tremendously over the past few years. Be sure to read the directions and follow them faithfully. If you use a rotary mower, it's time to change the blade. Alternate every month from now on through the season and keep the one not in use well sharpened, so it will be ready when you change next time.

Begin to mow in April or May, when your grass is well grown. Then, keep it cut at the best height to encourage turf growth and discourage weed infestations. Catch the clippings. Save them for your compost pile. Water regularly.

Believe me, if you follow the program above, or one similar to it, there is absolutely no reason why your lawn won't be the nicest, greenest grass anywhere.

Chapter 6.
Pickin' Berries and Squeezin' Grapes

Not so long ago, one of those so-called statistical experts told me that the average American doesn't eat as much fresh fruit as people who live in the warm climate countries of the world. When I think of all the apples, apricots, avocados, bananas, blueberries, blackberries, boysenberries, cantaloupes, cherries, cranberries, dates, dewberries, figs, fruit cocktails, guavas, grapes, grapefruit, gooseberries, honeydews, huckleberries, lemons, limes, loganberries, mangoes, muskmelons, nectarines, oranges, papayas, pawpaws, peaches, pears, prickly pears, prunes, quince jams, jellies, and pies, raisins, raspberries, rhubarb, strawberries, tangerines, tangelos, and watermelons I have eaten all over these United States in the last few years, I can only wonder if those warm climate folks aren't overdoing it?

I did a little research of my own and found out that, when you count frozen and canned fruit, we are the world's number one consumers. Each of us eats or drinks about 150 pounds of fruit each year.

Since the time of the Pilgrim Fathers, most American gardeners have included at least one or two fruits among their garden crops. I think you would be missing a bet (not to mention be unpatriotic) if you don't carry on that tradition.

Like most gardening projects, raising fruit crops is easy and fun. Don't think you don't have enough space, you can incorporate fruit crops into your landscaping plans whether you live in suburbia or a city apartment. Let's start our survey from the ground up with small fruits.

Rhubarb and Melons

I don't know why, but rhubarb isn't classed as a small fruit. Grandma called it "pie plant," and it's terrific stewed or mixed with strawberries in pies. This perennial is grown from root divisions. Look under vegetables. Melon cultivation will be found there too. If you live in the North, try New Hampshire Midget. However, these relatives of the squashes can pass for fruit any time. Mark Twain called watermelon "The food angels eat."

Strawberries

Strawberries are native to most parts of the world. No one knows who the first people were to cultivate wild strawberries, or even how they got their name. One story is that Anglo-Saxon children used to string them on straws and sell them. Whoever cultivated them first, American gardeners have inherited a tradition of growing them from the English. They are, hands down, our favorite berry fruit. In Izaak Walton's famous classic, *The Compleat Angler,* Dr. William Butler says, "Doubtless God could have made a better berry, but doubtless God never did." Those are my sentiments exactly!

It just may be, as someone once suggested, that the best-looking and most perfect-tasting strawberries grow only in our memory. They're the ones you may remember gathering from the wild on a sunny spring day. Or, they may be the ones you ate with shortcake and heavy cream, or ice cream, at a Country-Corners' annual strawberry social long ago. No matter how much truth there is to that idea, it isn't a good enough reason not to grow your own berries. Believe me, they will create the same kind of memories for all the members of your family.

How To Grow Strawberries

Most fruits are relatively easy to grow, but strawberries are the easiest. They can grow in just about any part of the country . . . and they do. They grow best in moist, well-drained soils. They need lots of water and good drainage. Check with your nurseryman to make sure the variety you are thinking of buying does well under your local growing conditions. By doing well, I mean they should have a record of producing at least one pint of fruit per plant the first year or fruiting season.

Locating and Preparing Your Patch

As I said, strawberries will grow almost anywhere, but it's best to avoid planting them where water stands above the ground in the winter or stays beneath the surface too long at any time of the year. If you do have a drainage problem, you can correct it by planting in raised beds. Just be sure to keep the soil moist.

When you locate your patch, keep it away from the roots and shade of large trees. Tree roots will take too much of the moisture from the soil and, in order to thrive, your berries will need full sun. They also need slightly acid soil and lots of food. Prepare your soil in the fall, before the snows come in the north or the rains in the south and west. For every hundred square feet of berry patch, apply fifty pounds of cattle manure and fifty pounds of leaves or leaf mold. Spade this mixture into the soil deeply. Top dress the bed with twenty-five pounds of gypsum per hundred square feet and let it set for the winter. This gypsum application will help loosen up heavy soil.

When spring comes, turn the soil again and grade off with a crown to allow good drainage. Check for weeds and remove any growing near the bed that might steal over into it. Now, apply three pounds of 10-6-4 lawn food per hundred square feet. Strawberry plants are like some people you know, they have big appetites and eat a lot. Feed them in the same proportions several times throughout the year. But you shouldn't feed them during fruiting time in the spring, or the plants will be so busy growing they'll produce poor quality fruit.

That All-Important "First Picking"

The first time you pick your berries is the most important. That's the time you pick which ones you are going to plant. Selecting the right varieties depends almost entirely on your growing needs. Alpine strawberries are perfect for edging flower beds and walks. They will produce good fruit from the end of June to the end of October.

The Shasta and Lassen varieties are the ones you will find most often on the produce counters of your supermarkets. California growers produce one-quarter of the world's crop with these varieties on only about 8,000 acres.

If flavor is the reason why you are growing strawberries, plant: Redglow, Red Rich, Fairfax, Ogallala, Ardmore, Sparkle, Ozark Beauty, Pocahontas, Midway, and Sunrise. Firmness is provided by: Dixieland, Surecrop, and Pocahontas. If you are looking for a high-yield crop, try: Catskill, Midway, Sunrise, Surecrop or Earlidawn.

Planting

Buy your plants from a reliable nursery, either in bare-root batches or potted individually. Try to plant whichever type you buy immediately. If that's not possible, store them in wet peat or in a trench dug in moist soil. Trim the bare-root type so that the roots are about three inches long. Plant your strawberries so the crown is just at surface level. This is critical. If the crown is too high, the roots will dry out; if too low, the crown will rot. Keep your newly planted strawberries well-watered until you're sure they are doing well.

Plant your berries in the early spring. It's all right to plant in the fall, before the first frost, if you live in a mild climate like California. Never plant them after July 15th in snow country.

If you are planting a fairly large crop, space your rows two to three feet apart. You can plant in single, double, or triple rows. Plants should have one foot of growing space on either side. Strawberries you set out in April will begin to blossom in May. You should pick off all these buds and blossoms as soon as they appear. When the plants start to send out runners, clip them off. You want your strawberries to be able to concentrate on producing fruit.

Your strawberries should be heavily mulched. You can plant them through soggy newspaper as described in an earlier chapter, or mulch them with clean straw. Pine needles also make a good mulch material because of their acid content. The mulch will hold down the weeds and inhibit runner growth. In the late fall, just before the first frost, build up your mulch to three or four inches between rows and cover the plants. If your area is accustomed to mild winters, leave some of the foliage showing through the mulch.

Making New Plants From Runners

To create new plants from those you previously planted, use the layering system as you would with other berry crops. Cover long runners with soil allowing several inches on the end to stick out above ground. When the buried portion takes root, clip it off. Then take up a good portion of the soil around it when you replant.

Grandma's Strawberry Patch

Grandma Putt had a strawberry patch that produced big, fat, juicy berries year after year. She washed her berry plants with soap and water to ward off disease and insects. She said that many people go wrong raising strawberries because they expected too much of them. Don't assume just because strawberries are perennials that they will go on producing good fruit forever. And, don't expect that you can develop new plants from runners indefinitely. These secondary plants tend to produce smaller and harder berries after a few years. The plants will be more susceptible to disease. The secret of always getting big berries is to keep rotating your stock. Introduce newly purchased berries into your patch every year. Eliminate old plants every two or three years.

An Old-Fashioned Strawberry Barrel

If you live where space is a problem and you still want to grow strawberries, get yourself an old barrel and remake it into a concentrated berry patch. The barrel can be cedar, oak, or redwood. From about a foot from the ground, cut three- or four-inch holes spaced about every ten inches. Drill a good-sized hole in the bottom of the barrel for drainage. Make a cylindrical collar about four to six inches in diameter and place it down the center of the barrel. Fill this collar with sand and gravel. Surround the collar with planter's mix and peat moss. Plant your strawberry plants, one per hole. Set your barrel on a sunny apartment balcony or a sunny patio. It's a good idea to place the barrel on some sort of castered platform so you can turn it every so often to the sun. Bring it inside in the winter. See that it is kept well-watered and gets plenty of light—either sunlight or flourescent Vita-Lite or Sylvania Gro-Lux.

Wild Strawberries

One of the real treats of a trip to Fowler's Woods in late spring or early summer, was a visit to my favorite wild strawberry patch. Wild strawberries are really special. I once asked Grandma why wild strawberries taste so much better than the ones that folks grow in berry patches. She laughed and said it was because Mother Earth is a better gardener than most folks. Wild strawberries are usually smaller than the garden-grown varieties but they are much sweeter and their leaves have a great deal of nutritional value as salad spinach. If you and your family ever have a chance to go berrying for wild strawberries, don't pass it up.

Brambleberries

Anyone who has ever wandered into a patch of wild brambleberries has probably carried away as many scars as berries! Brambleberries include: blackberries, boysenberries, dewberries, loganberries, red and yellow raspberries.

Blackberries

Grandma Putt said that Americans were probably the only people with enough fortitude to cultivate blackberries. Most Europeans considered the blackberry a worthless weed. But if you had ever tasted Grandma's blackberry flummery, made with fresh-picked Darrows, you'd appreciate their true worth as a small fruit. Blackberries come in two main types; erect or semi-erect, and the trailing type. This last type are commonly called dewberries.

The erect and semi-erect types, which grow from Maine to Nebraska and in the South and Far West, include the following varieties:

Bailey	Humble
Darrow	Smoothstem
Early Harvest	Thornfree
Early Wonder	

Trailing varieties include:

Lucretia	Young or
Jerseyblack	Youngberry

Boysenberries, a trailing type are sometimes classified as a separate kind of berry. With loganberries, they are the two berries developed in this country in this century. Boysenberry pie is one of the highlights of a visit to Walter Knott's Berry Farm in Buena Park, California. Mr. Knott is credited with the commercial development of the boysenberry.

Growing Blackberries

Plant your blackberries three inches deeper than they were grown. Cut the tops back to twelve inches and place the plants three feet apart.

Don't plant blackberries where any of their cousins, or tomatoes, potatoes, or eggplant have grown previously. These plants are all susceptible to some of the same rust and virus diseases. Keep the soil well cultivated until July. For best results, keep plants five to six feet apart. You will probably want to plant at least a half-dozen plants if you have a large family as each blackberry plant produces about a quart of berries per year. Don't expect berries the first year, but you should have plenty the second. Blackberry bushes last about ten years on an average and should produce well from the second year on.

PRUNING

From the second year on, you will need to prune your blackberry plants. The best time to do this is in early spring. Snip off the weakest canes, also any weak or dead lateral branches. A procedure called "pinching off" will be necessary in the summer. This means you should pinch off the growing tips of all shoots over two and a half feet. This will cause them to branch out and be ready to bear fruit. After the fruit has been completely picked, cut out the canes that bore berries and you will be all ready for the next year.

In the case of the trailing-type berries, spring pruning is minimal. Remove the weak canes and cut the healthy ones back to five or six feet. After harvest, cut out the ones that bore fruit.

MULCHING AND FEEDING

To eliminate weeds, mulch your berry plants with pine needles or bark. Put your mulch on as soon as the hot weather weed-growing season and keep it on until the following spring. At that time you will want to remove it to cultivate around the plants.

I feed my blackberries with 10-6-4 liquid lawn food. Use about a cupful for each plant every spring and a handful of balanced dry fertilizer in mid-August.

SPRAYING

Spray with a general purpose fruit spray just prior to and right after the fruiting period.

Raspberries

There are red, yellow, and black or purple raspberries. They come in summer-bearing and ever-bearing varieties. Raspberries are more commonly grown in home gardens than blackberries and you will be able to find varieties suited for almost any regional climate in the country. However, most raspberries prefer growing where there are long and cool springs.

Prepare your raspberry planting bed as you would for strawberries or blackberries. Try to find a spot that's sheltered. Plant as directed for blackberries in full sun and as early in the spring as possible. These plants can take a little late frost and, if planted early enough, will be ready to bear fruit in the fall. Most nursery stock is about one year old. Feed and mulch like blackberries. Like trailing blackberries, raspberries will need some support—especially during the fruiting period. You can stake them up with cedar poles, which are available at most nurseries or lumberyards; or, if you planted in rows, place stakes at the ends of each row and run wires down either side of the plants. Be ruthless in eliminating suckers that spring up between plants unless you want to transplant the more healthy of these as new plants. Raspberries don't tend to spread as much as blueberries so you only need allow three to four feet between plants. After harvesting the mid-summer bearing varieties, cut off the canes that bore fruit at ground level. If your plants are the ever-bearing type, cut off the tips of canes that bore fruit. These same canes may bear heavier fruit next season.

My favorite raspberries include: Canby and Taylor in the reds; Amber in the yellow; Bristol and Starking Black Giant in the black, and Sodus in the purple. Berry growers say it's not good to mix red and black in the same berry patch. And don't plant one where the other used to grow.

The Bush Berries

Several kinds of sweet and spicy berries are grown and cultivated on bushes. Among the best known of these are blueberries, huckleberries, currants, gooseberries, elderberries, and serviceberries (or shadbush plums). All are perennials.

Blueberries

Blueberries were once so common all over the world that people just took them for granted and never grew them in their gardens. They are probably the easiest wild fruit to name because they seem to be native to every part of the world. They are eaten by Eskimos at the Arctic Circle and Indians in the South American jungles, but only here in the United States and Canada are they raised commercially or in home gardens. That's because U.S. and Canadian blueberries are getting sweeter and bigger and better every year. Blueberries have been tremendously improved by horticulturists over the past two decades.

They are much more easily grown than anyone ever suspected. Even when I lived with Grandma Putt, it was very common to let blueberries grow in the wild. And most folks did their pickin' up on Blueberry Hill.

You will find these are pretty easy fellows to cope with . . . so plant some bushes and enjoy the luscious results! Grow blueberries in full sun. They require moist soil, and plenty of water. They prefer a slightly acid soil, but will thrive even where the soil is in a neutral pH condition. Prepare your soil in the fall with well-rotted manure and humus as I described for strawberries. In the spring, two weeks before planting, apply a commercial fertilizer with a high nitrogen content, or use an evergreen fertilizer recommended for azaleas.

Once every two or three years, cut out the old wood to allow new branches and foliage to grow. I recommend you do this early in the spring before the plants begin blooming. Aside from that, mulch well with pine needles and get your blueberry buckets ready. You should have a bumper crop. Plant enough bushes in close proximity to each other, so that they will cross-pollinate. Plants are usually sold in groupings of six or more for just this purpose. Unless you want to be a living scarecrow, you'd better get some close fish netting for when the berries come. Otherwise, your blueberries will be for the birds!

Here are some recommended varieties: Concord, Rubel, Jersey, Bluecrop, Dixi, and Pemberton; early varieties include: Earliblue and Collins; rabbit-eye varieties like Tifblue. These grow slightly larger bushes than the standard or highbush varieties above.

Huckleberries

In the Middle West, from Michigan to Mark Twain country, kids grew up calling blueberries, huckleberries, and vice versa. Actually there is a difference. Huckleberries grow only in the wild. They are just a little bit smaller than true blues and have large, hard seeds. I still can't tell the difference between wild blueberries and wild huckleberries. I wonder if Huckleberry Finn could?

Gooseberries and Currants

Grandma Putt made currant jelly and gooseberry pie. Those are just two good reasons to consider growing currants and gooseberries! These spicy bush berries grow well in the northern part of the United States and in Canada. You'll find them under cultivation and growing wild in New England, the Appalachians, the Great Lakes states, the Dakotas, the Mountain states and in the cool Pacific coast states of Washington and Oregon.

IMPORTANT! Some states outlaw new plantings because these plants often are "carriers" of one stage of the blister-rust fungus which kills large numbers of the white pine tree. Check with your local forestry department or state department of agriculture before planting. Any nurseryman worth his spade should know if they are permitted in your area.

187

HOW TO GROW

Currants and gooseberries are self-fruiting. Purchase two-year-old plants. Cut long roots off and set three feet apart. Cut tops back to six inches. Set new plants one to two inches deeper than they were previously planted. That means about a half foot deep. Your two-year-old cuttings should bear fruit the following year.

For red currants I like: Red Lake, Perfection, Cascade, and Boskoop Giant; for the white variety, try White Imperial; horticulturists have been working to find a currant that's highly resistant or immune to the blister-rust fungus: Viking may be the answer. European gooseberries like Fredonia grow best in Washington state and Oregon. They have the best-tasting fruit, but are disease-prone. Charles Downing is the variety of gooseberry I know best. You can also try Chautauqua early, and Pixwell.

Keep currants pruned. February or early March is the best pruning time. Cut off canes older than three years.

Giving your currants and gooseberries a soap-and-water shower twice a month, from spring to autumn, will help them ward off fungus and other less persistent diseases and pests.

Another showering procedure recommended by old-timers is an alkaline wash with diluted lime water . . . both on the tops and bottoms of leaves. Apply in the spring. This should ward off the blight and mildew. Spade some wood ashes or agricultural charcoal in around the base in the late fall.

Both currants and gooseberries are usually very disease resistant. They need sun, but prefer the north shady side of a hill. Gooseberries are good for pies. I remember that from my childhood, but once Ilene decided to "give me a treat" and bake one. The berries seemed a little sour while she was preparing them for the filling. By the time she was finished, she had used nearly two pounds of sugar and the pie turned out so sour even my kids (who will eat anything labeled "dessert") turned it down . . . and so did the dog. There must be a secret to baking a delicious gooseberry pie. If you find out what it is, let me know.

Elderberries

Next to blueberries, the elderberry is the commonest wild fruit-bearing shrub in America. During Prohibition, elderberries became more and more popular as a cultivated shrub. They have very pretty blossoms which appear in June and July. And these very pretty blossoms have been known to make a very tasty wine. The berries are also used for wine—and for jams and jellies. The bushes are available from many nurseries and are easy to grow. Plant them in a sunny location in the fall or early spring.

Juneberries or Shadbush Plums

These grow all over New England and out in the Northwest where they are known as serviceberries. The berries can be eaten uncooked and range in color from red to purple. Some eastern varieties grow into good-looking blossoming trees that rival the white dogwood in attractiveness. Juneberry jelly and shad-plum pie are part of our early American cooking tradition. They need lots of water and a shady spot to grow in.

Other Berries and Small Fruit

If you want to attract some birds to your garden, plant sugarberry, mulberry, chokecherry, or barberry trees and shrubs. There are twenty edible varieties of hawthorn and they make a fine ornamental. Paul's Scarlet is my favorite. We have one, but I don't know whether its bright red fall fruit makes good jelly. Ground cherries are not cherries at all. They have been found in gardens and nursery catalogues for more than a hundred years. I've never tried them, but everyone who has says the fruit is delicious. Grow as an annual vegetable or an ornamental. The plants are free-fruiting and will grow in any good garden soil. Set out in early spring and pick when ripe. You can dry in the husks what you don't eat.

Cranberries

With corn, squash, beans, pumpkins, etc., cranberries are a part of our American tradition. Nobody knows for sure, but it has always been pretty much taken for granted that cranberries were eaten with turkey on the first Thanksgiving. That idea was sold to the public so hard that it has hurt the commercial turkey and cranberry business. Now it's hard to get folks to eat them other than during the holiday season.

I don't know anyone who grows cranberries in their home garden. Most new homeowners complain about the quality of the land their homes were built on, but few of us have bogs suitable for growing cranberries.

If you live in an area where cranberries are grown and want to try them, talk to a commercial grower for tips. The bogs can usually be filled or drained of water easily so the growers can control the temperature.

The flowers are white or pale-rose and are said to resemble cranes. And that is how the berries got their name. They appear in the summer and are green, but by late September or October turn bright red. Growers recommend Hawes or Early Blacks as good varieties for cultivation.

Grapes

Grandma Putt wasn't what you would call a wino, but she knew how to make apple, dandelion, elderberry, rose, and grape wines. Her grapes were Concords and her wine was sweet. She always said it made a better dessert than a main course. But more than wine, there were plenty of other culinary delights connected with Grandma's grapes. One of my favorites was Concord grape pie, not to mention grape jelly and, of course, a luscious bunch of grapes for eating on a crisp September day.

The Psalm says, "Wine maketh glad the heart of man," and there have been glad hearts somewhere in the world every night for more than six thousand years. Wine is known to have been used in the earliest records of man. The Greeks first brought the grape to the Western world and the Egyptians were the Gallo Brothers of ancient times.

If the bubonic plague hadn't wiped out the people in Iceland in the fourteenth century (and with them, the memory of North America's discovery), we all might be "Vinlanders" instead of Americans. The early Norse voyagers saw so many huge grape vines growing along the Canadian and New England coast, they dubbed this continent "Wineland." If the name had stuck, we might be a nation of winos. As it is, we *are* a nation of wine drinkers. *Time* magazine estimates that Americans will have spent $2,000,000,000 for wine last year (1972), and the future looks grapier and grapier. *Time* says at 2.4 gallons a year, we'll have to do a lot more wining than dining to catch up to the French who drink 29 gallons and the Italians who drink 30 gallons a year. At the risk of being called an American Firster I believe we can do it.

Growing Grapes

The four cedar-post trellises for Grandma's grapes ran parallel to each other for about twenty feet on the southwest corner of her yard. Behind them was the chicken coop. To the south (and a great distance from the house) was the hog pen. Her grapeyard, as she called it, was a tiny, thriving vineyard in its own right.

Her trellises ran north and south in good fertile soil, but I have since learned, from several good authorities, grapes prefer a southern exposure in moist, slightly acid soil.

Grapes can be propagated from cuttings which you purchase from a nursery or from a spring pruning of established vines—or by layering one-year-old shoots. In any of these three cases, plant them right away or store them in wet sand until winter and then plant in the spring.

You can incorporate grapes into your landscape plan by espaliering them against a sunny wall of your house or garage (I even saw a vine-covered outhouse once). Or, train them to an arbor.

But if you want grapes for eating and preserving instead of grapes for looking at, build some grape trellises. Here's how to do it.

LONG CANE TRELLISING:

Planting your vine before building your trellis is like putting the cart before the horse. Pound 8 or 10 foot 2 x 4 cedar posts 2 or 3 feet into the ground every 10 feet for a distance of, say, 20 feet. Between this row of posts, string large-gauge wire (10 gauge is preferable) at a height of 30 inches and at 60 inches. Use adjustable wire tighteners to make the wires taut. Now plant your cuttings along the trellis. They should be planted 8 inches deep and 5 feet apart.

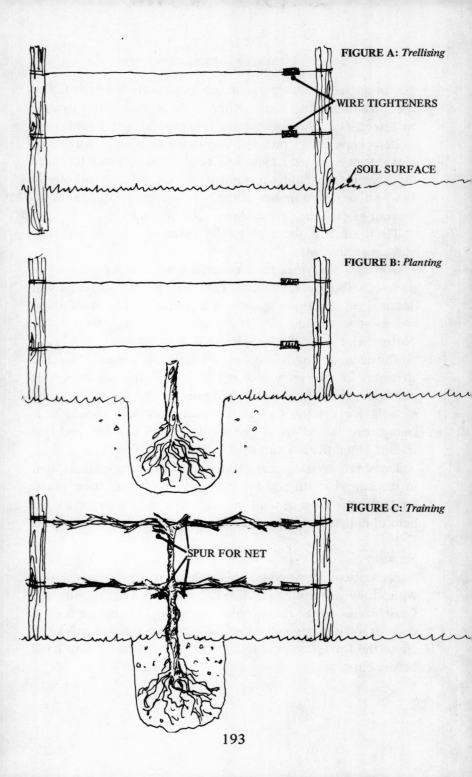

FIGURE A: *Trellising*

WIRE TIGHTENERS

SOIL SURFACE

FIGURE B: *Planting*

FIGURE C: *Training*

SPUR FOR NET

Put in enough to hedge your bet against those which fail to root. When planting rooted nursery stock, place them every 6 to 8 feet. Dig a hole about 2½ feet around and 1 foot deep.

Before planting, mix the dug-out soil equally with well-rotted compost, peat moss and bone meal or a well-balanced mild fertilizer. Hand pack a little mound of this mixture in the bottom 6 to 8 inches of the hole and spread out the roots of your grape cane over it. Now, refill the hole.

Tie the top of the cane to the lower wire of the trellis or stake it to that wire.

Getting your vines to produce a good crop of grapes is a three- to four-year process. The first year, your cane will develop two or three shoots. Select the healthiest of these and tie it to the top wire. If it's not long enough, tie it to the bottom wire. This will become your main vine.

The second year, when the lateral shoots appear, allow the strongest four to grow. Cut off all the others, but leave four bud spurs (Figure C) which will produce the following year's growth. By the third or fourth year, your vine should have four strong lateral arms: two trained to the top wire and two trained along the bottom wire (Figure C).

There are several other planting and trellising systems used in the humid south and far north. If you live in these areas, contact your local agricultural school or extension service for helpful bulletins on grape growing.

PRUNING

Prune your grape vines in the late winter or early spring while they are dormant. As with most pruning, be ruthless. Grandma said that this pruning must be done before the sap rises or your vines will bleed. If you must wait until later, allow the leaves to grow to the size of the palm of your hand before cutting.

GRAPE LEAVES

Two things I want to mention about grape leaves. First, don't make the mistake of pulling leaves off to expose hidden bunches of grapes to the sun. The grapes do need sun, but the leaves manufacture much of their sugar. When you pinch off leaves, your grapes may become acid-tasting.

Second, ask anyone from the Middle East or Greece, and they'll tell you that grape leaves are good eating. Check your cookbooks, ladies!

MILDEW

Grandma applied sulphur dust to the woody parts of her vines to ward off the mildew.

VARIETIES

Selecting the proper varieties of grapes is crucial. Since the first settlers, growers have learned to their dismay that climate is the key to growing certain types of grapes. For instance, Thomas Jefferson tried and failed to grow European wine grapes at Mt. Vernon. Hundreds of doubting Thomases before and since have tried the same thing with the same dismal results. In general, bunch grapes grow best in the North, Midwest, Southeast, and Far West. Wine grapes do well in northern California and muscadine grapes do well all along the Pacific Coast and down into Texas.

Here is a partial list of varieties for each of the three groups:

Bunch Grapes. These are descendants of those fox grapes the Norsemen saw:

Beta	Interlaken Seedless
Blue Lake	Isabella
Brighton	Moore Early

Catawba	Niagra
Concord	Norton
Delaware	Ontario
Ellen Scott	Portland
Fredonia	Seneca
Golden Muscat	Van Buren

Muscadine. These are the grapes you see in your stores in the fall:

Burgaw	Scuppernong
Dearing	Thomas
Hunt	Topsail
Magoon	

Wine Grapes. American wine is just beginning to come into its own both here and abroad. Most of the varieties listed below were either brought to California by the Franciscans or were introduced in the middle of the nineteenth century. Most of them are grown commercially, but if you live in California wine country or in some parts of the Southwest and can get cuttings, go ahead. A quarter of a million Americans make their own wine at home. The federal government allows up to 200 gallons, so good growing and good cheer!

Alicante Bouschet	Pinot Noir
Flame	Seibel 5279
Johannesberg Riesling	Zinfandel
Muscat of Alexandria	

European Table Grapes. Some of these can be used for wine:

196

Black Monukka
Cardinal
Csaba
Delight
Exotic

Muscat Hamburg
Perlette
Seibel 5279
Thompson Seedless

SUMMARY

With all grapes it pays to learn all you can about the varieties you plan to grow. Consult the Department of Agriculture, state and local agriculture extension services and agricultural schools in your area. Varieties differ as to growing climate and in other ways. Some grapes are self-unfruitful. Specific varieties ripen early, mid-season and late. Certain varieties even have specific seasons. I recommend you get all the information you can before you begin.

Figs

We never grew figs except as small ornamental trees. They are truly one of Mother Nature's most beautiful works of art. Good fruit varieties include: Celeste, Everbearing, Green Ischia, Hunt, Kadota, Mission, and Southeastern Brown Turkey. These can be grown just as easily as grapes in the South and Southwest. Newer bush-type varieties make cultivation possible in parts of the North. Give them constant sun and protect them from cold and wet weather. Tie the branches together for winter and mulch wild straw, leaves or leaf mold. Take one of those big plastic trash bags, turn it upside down and cover plants, mulch and all. Then, mulch around and up over the bottom. If you live where it gets below 50°, plant in tubs and take inside over the winter. Fig trees can be grown from eight to ten inch cuttings similar to grapes. Root the cuttings in sand or you can use layering techniques as with raspberries.

Prune them severely after harvest. New fruit appears on new growth like the berries and grapes.

If you have dry soil, water regularly. Mulch with compost. In the South and Southwest harvest should begin in July.

A Small-Fruit-Grower's Calendar

SPRING

1. As soon as severe frosts are over, you can begin preparing your soil, then, planting.

2. Sandy or gravel soils can be worked immediately after a rain.

3. Heavy soil should not be worked when it's too wet or too dry.

4. Plant as early as you possibly can, but make sure the soil is friable (crumbly). Don't plant on a windy day . . . especially a cold windy day. If you can, get your plants in before the spring rains. They will gain moisture and nitrogen. Remember, planting earth should be moist not wet and soggy.

5. If you have an extremely dry spring, soak your berry patch thoroughly in the morning and plant that evening. Never let roots get dry or shrivel. If roots are frozen, let them dry out in the garage or basement before planting.

6. Shorten strawberry roots one-third and grape cane roots to six inches before planting.

7. If roots smell musty . . . wash them in warm clean water.

8. When planting (anytime of year) don't let roots touch unrotted manure or burning fertilizer of any kind.

9. If you water at all, do it thoroughly and keep your fruit and berry plants wet until the rains come. Sporadic watering is worse than no watering.

10. Watch your plants carefully just as you do young children in springtime. This is when unexpected cold and heavy rains or frosts can bring on sickness. Turn your back on your living young plants too long and you may find them destroyed by disease when you turn around.

11. When you have just set strawberry plants, *don't* cultivate heavily near the roots. Use a rake and just stir the surface not more than 1/2 inch deep.

12. Mulch as soon as you can and heavily with pine needles, old newspapers, straw, etc. Mulch only moist ground. Dry ground covered with mulch will stay dry.

SUMMER

1. Late spring and early summer is the time to do pruning and "pinching off." Do this while plants are still in their spring and summer growth and not when the wood begins to ripen.

2. Late pruning of grape vines should take place when the leaves are the size of the palm of your hand.

3. In early summer, rake the ground in your berry patch once a week. This will destroy the weeds and keep the ground moist.

4. Keep your mulch up and heavy. It, too, will keep heat and weeds out and moisture in. Again, don't mulch dry ground.

5. Pick fruit, if possible, when it is dry and in the cool parts of the day.

6. Don't leave just-picked fruit in the sun. Take it to a cool shady spot immediately.

FALL
1. Top-dress all small fruit on your property with compost mixed with bone meal or any delayed-release fertilizer. Spread it along the rows. Cultivate it in just above the roots where it does the most good.

2. This is also the time to eliminate all perennial weeds that may have gotten into your berry patch. Be careful not to disturb strawberry roots, as exposure to the winter frost will kill them.

3. If you have a heavy spring gardening agenda, save some of that precious time now by planting blackberries, currants, gooseberries, and raspberries. Check your nursery to make sure the varieties you select can be fall-planted. Planting can't take place until these fruits have dropped their fall foliage.

4. Do as much soil preparation in the fall as you can. Spring is always too short to get everything you want to do done.

5. If your soil is heavy and you plan to plant it in the spring, plow, roto-till, or spade it deeply. Go back over the furrows to make them deeper. This exposes your berry patch or vineyard, to what is called "winter-heaving" . . . making it more workable in the spring. It also exposes insects and their larvae to the killing winter freezes.

6. If your soil is light and sandy, don't spade or till it in the fall, unless you want to plow under a cover crop of green manure to add humus.

WINTER

1. Just as the ground is about to freeze, cover strawberry plants with a mulch material that will prevent freezing and thawing during the coldest part of winter. Leaves, straw, hay, *light* manure, or garden litter are fine for this job.

2. You can continue to plant brambleberries on mild winter days when there is no frost in the air or in the soil. Surround the roots with plenty of the planting mix recommended earlier. Frozen earth should never come into contact with the roots.

3. In the early winter, write for new nursery catalogues and plan your spring fruit crops.

4. Check your tools. Clean and mend those that need either.

5. When your fruit catalogues arrive, study them carefully. Don't let all those pretty pictures lure you into buying more work this winter than you can handle next spring and summer.

6. Winter ashes from your fireplace should be saved for applying on your fruit plantings.

7. Late winter is the time for pruning of grape vines. Be sure to do this before the sap rises. Otherwise, your vines will bleed profusely. Grape vine sap doesn't clot like people's blood.

Chapter 7.
Eatin' Apple Pie
and Other Tasties

Living out in the country, near a small town, it seemed as if there was always some sort of fruit being harvested. It is amazing how important an effect these fruit harvests had on everyone's social life. When the berries were ripe, kids, adults, and young lovers went berry-pickin'. Then there were Strawberry, Raspberry, and Blueberry Socials. There was the Cherry Pie Sale put on by the P.T.A. at the school. Grapes went into jellies, conserves, and pies and these wound up as the highlight of some church supper. Any big community doings was topped off with peach pie and ice cream or deep-dish apple pie with melted cheese. So many apples were carried to school, I'm sure the teachers gave away all except the prettiest and tastiest. We bobbed for apples, we ate taffy-apples and mothers made doughnuts to eat with apples and cider around the huge bonfires the dads lit almost every night during the fall. Who says there were no "good old days"?

The Large Fruits

None of your plants will pay back the care you give them as abundantly as your large fruit trees. Sadly, home gardeners and even some farmers tend to ignore these beautiful and bountiful botanical buddies. I'm not going to suggest you plant an orchard. Most people can't spare the land or the time, nor can they cope with the kind of a harvest ten or twenty standard fruit trees will produce! Modern refrigeration, storage methods and transportation have made most large fruit too easily available. Even two standard-size apple trees will provide enough ingredients to make more apple pies and apple pandowdy than most mothers are prepared to bake. Still, there's nothing like biting into a crisp sweet or spicy apple you grew yourself.

Grandma's Fruit Trees

Grandma Putt had her fruit trees pretty well integrated into her landscaping. But, her apple trees were back up against a neighbor's orchard. His name was Roy States, and when it came time to care for his trees. he took care of Grandma's at the same time. What he didn't do to make the trees produce better, his bees did for him. It seemed like there were always plenty of apples, either on the tree, on the ground, or in barrels and bushel baskets down in Grandma's root cellar. For this we could partly thank Roy, and partly his bees.

Honey bees and other insects will become best friends to you and your fruit trees. Many varieties of apples, apricots, cherries, peaches, pears, and plums are self-unfruitful. That means, they can't set fruit without help from a tree of the same variety growing nearby. The two trees are cross-pollinated by flying insects or ants.

A Revolution in Fruit Tree Size and Production

In the past twenty years or so, something has happened that makes large fruit production possible for those of us who have only the smallest amount of land. This has been the widespread introduction of semi-dwarf, dwarf, and double-dwarf fruit trees.

A standard apple tree, for instance, grows 20 to 25 feet high and 25 to 35 feet wide at the tallest and widest part of its foliage. The spur-type semi-dwarf tree grows only 12 to 15 feet high and 12 to 15 feet wide. Stark Nurseries (the world's largest grower of fruit trees) says you can plant 200 semi-dwarf trees on the same acre that used to take only 40 standard trees. And, you can get just about the same amount of fruit per tree, as the semi-dwarfs set fruit all throughout the foliage, while the standards set fruit only on the outside perimeter of the foliage.

Newer dwarf-type trees are the result of a chance discovery. A dwarf crabapple tree was found growing in nature in Iowa. Researchers at Iowa State University used twigs from this tree to turn a normal standard type tree into a potential dwarf by grafting. These trees, which grew to a height of about 8 feet, produced standard-sized fruit. Now, dwarf trees have been developed which produce larger fruit than standard trees. The latest development from Stark's is a series of double-dwarf varieties which, they say, will alter the shape of apple orchards as we have known them. These trees grow 6 to 10 feet tall, and set large fruit and bear very young. I recommend these trees for folks with small yards or serious space problems. They can be trained on wires and as espalier-type trees.

Landscaping with Fruit Trees

Every time someone asks me for landscaping advice, I tell them not to overlook the ornamental beauty and shade provided by fruit trees. In almost every part of the country, there are several fruit types and varieties which will grow well, look beautiful, and produce tasty crops. Almost all fruit trees have attractive shapes and are covered with fragrant and beautiful flowers for at least a week or more before they bear their fruit. Select a size that fits into your landscape best.

Espaliering

Training fruit trees to grow in espalier patterns is a time-honored gardening art form that comes to us from ancient Persia and medieval Europe. As I mentioned, dwarf trees are especially adaptable to artistic training of this sort. Spring planting is best, but you can plant canned or balled-in-burlap trees for your living fence in the fall where winters begin early and are severe. Temperatures should get down to at least 10°. If winters in your area have alternate thaws and freezes, do not plant in the fall or your trees will get off to a weakened start. I suggest locating your "fence-row" and preparing the soil as one of your fall gardening projects.

Be sure there are no underground tiles, pipes or electrical work that will interfere with proper root growth. First, dig a 2 x 2 foot trench and take out all the soil. Fill the bottom 3 inches with a liberal quantity of bone meal or any mild slow-releasing garden food. Mix in 25 pounds of peat moss and 25 pounds of compost, leaves, or leaf-mold for every 50 feet of "fence-row." When these materials are thoroughly mixed, shovel them back into the trench and cover the top two inches with gypsum. Allow to set during the winter.

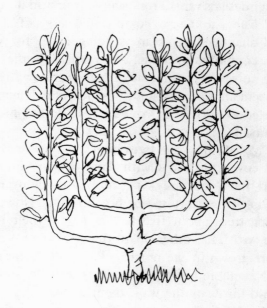

209

Espalier designs range from simple four-arm designs used in grape trellising, to a more complicated series of "U," "V," or diamond shapes. If you are sending away for your trees, include a copy of your design and a note with the order. That way, the nurseryman filling it can select trees with the proper limb placement to make your design work. It may be best if there's a good nursery in your area, to go and pick out your trees yourself.

When you bring your trees home or they arrive from the nursery, cover the roots with damp burlap or cloth. Make sure that the roots are kept moist until you are ready to plant. Clip off any bruised or broken roots. Now, plant your espaliering trees about five feet apart, so their roots won't interfere with each other. Plant them two inches deeper than they were grown in the nursery. Place the fertile soil around the roots so there are no air pockets. Fill the soil firmly for about two-thirds of the way, then fill the sides so there is a saucer-like depression near the trench to catch the rain. The graft or bud union should be just *above* the surface of the soil after planting. This is an important rule in planting dwarf trees. If this entire union is below the surface, the part of the graft above the union will take root and you'll lose the dwarfing characteristic. Mulch around your newly planted tree with newspaper shreds, straw, or bark. You should water at least once a week, unless there is a heavy rain.

How to Train Your Espalier Design

Select only springy, healthy branches for training. They will have to be tied to some sort of secure and sturdy support for at least two years. Use a strong lattice fence or trellising as described for grapes. Tie them to the support with pieces of old nylon hose. Never make such sharp bends that your branch wood cracks or tears. If it does wrinkle up, bind it with cloth bandage material and paint with tree wound dressing.

Don't prune off all unwanted limbs the first year. Extra branches and foliage you are not using for training will help the young tree develop a healthy root system. Don't feed your tree this first year either. Transplanted trees grow entirely on water the first year in their new surroundings. In the years ahead, though, they'll enjoy all that rich, fertile soil where you planted them. The first time the trees bear, it's probably a good idea to pick off the fruit as its weight may destroy all your training pains. Cut off all suckers unless you need a particularly healthy sucker to replace a trained limb that has been damaged. Tie the sucker along the damaged limb until it begins to take, then cut the old unwanted limb off.

Planting Standard-Sized Fruit Trees

Prepare soil for standard trees as you would for espalier dwarfs. Most standard-sized fruit trees need plenty of room for their roots to roam. Allow about fifteen to twenty feet. Don't plant them too close to driveways, or you will find out that Mother Nature gives them the strength to break up concrete. Also, don't plant standard trees too close to buildings or under caves or telephone wires. You don't want some hurried lineman hacking off your tree's upper limbs. Plant as you would dwarf trees, except this time the bud union should be just *under* the soil. If you did not prepare the soil for spring planting the previous fall, don't use the soil from the hole when you plant your fruit tree. Instead, use a commercial planting mix like Cornell University's Redi-Mix. Dig the hole for standard trees a foot and a half deep and two and a half feet wide. Stake newly planted trees. All fruit trees should be staked and protected against the winter weather or gnawing by rodents. This is especially necessary for young cherry trees. Alternate winter freezes and thaws can make the bark split on young trees at the soil surface. They need protective coverings and a high mulch. Throw tarps or old blankets over dwarf trees if there is an unseasonable freeze due. Use wire mesh or similar protective material around the base, and a tree wrap you can purchase at any nursery for preventing freeze-up or sun-scald. If you live where there are moderate to heavy winds, stake up your tree by driving a pipe or two-by-two about six inches from the trunk. Run some· wire through two pieces of old rubber hose and fasten to the tree.

Apples Are Easy to Get Along With

I don't know who is credited with inventing it, but there is nothing more traditionally American than apple pie . . . unless, of course, it's made with Russian apples! Actually, apples originated in southwestern Asia and are now native to most parts of the world. Varieties have been cultivated and highly developed in Europe, Russia, South Africa, Australia, Korea, China, India, South America, and elsewhere . . . probably everywhere but the Garden of Eden, where the apple that caused all the trouble is now believed by Biblical scholars to have been an apricot. But, as widespread and cultivated as the apple may be elsewhere, no country had adopted it more thoroughly and wholeheartedly than ours. Back in the 1800s, developing new apple varieties in the U.S.

was such a popular garden hobby, that cataloguers couldn't keep up. At one time, there were an estimated two thousand varieties growing here!

Apples are easy to grow. They are healthy and hardy. This country often grows enough apples in a year to provide a bushel of the fruit for every man, woman, and child who lives here. Your apple tree likes heavy feeding, but will put up with low feeding and sometimes even no feeding. Is your land too rocky? Plant apple trees! They are almost indifferent to soil and exposure.

Feeding and Watering

Roy watered his fruit trees during the hottest, driest days of summer or during unseasonable droughts. Otherwise, they never saw the hose. When you do water, soak the ground thoroughly out to the weep line. Sporadic and uneven watering is next to useless.

Your trees have to put out a great deal of effort in order to bear fruit. Just as your appetite increases during periods of hard, physical labor, so is it with fruit trees.

After the first year, feed your young trees in the spring and fall. A 4-12-4 or 5-10-5 garden food will suit your purposes just fine. Scatter five pounds of this food out to the weep line and water in thoroughly.

You'll notice, when your trees reach middle age their appetites increase according to the amount of fruit they produce. Double the amount of your spring and fall feedings to ten pounds each time.

Then, when your faithful fruit trees reach their golden years and old age, they will need all the help they can get to bear what they can. Give them fifteen pounds of food in the spring and in the fall.

Thinning

Thinning your fruit trees often improves the size of succeeding crops. Grandma and Roy often argued about when this should be done. Roy said twenty days after trees reach full bloom. Grandma always waited until the trees dropped their fruit naturally in the spring windfalls (orchardists call this the "spring drop"). She said this was Mother Nature's thinning. She said we should help Mother Nature if she got too busy and forgot.

Pruning

You should prune your fruit trees to keep the trees thin enough so they won't break down under a heavy crop of fruit. Prune them high enough so your budding Isaac Newtons can sit under them to think. When your trees are young, prune them severely to form what is called a "head." Prune thin and leave five or seven branches evenly distributed around the main stem and cut back to this main stem at least one-third. Be careful not to allow two branches to grow directly opposite each other. This causes forking and creates a weak spot where the wood might split. If thorough pruning is done in the first two seasons, little will be needed thereafter. Prune apples, cherries, pears, quinces, European plums so they develop a central leader with alternate side branches; trim peaches and Japanese plums so they grow low by cutting back the leader and all side branches; cherries, pears, and plums usually don't require much pruning after planting. Dwarf trees are pruned in the same way as standards.

When you receive your fruit trees from the nursery, remove any excess growth missed by the nurseryman. Select five to seven well-spaced branches that will develop into a good head. For the first two or three years, remove fruit before it develops. Give your dwarf trees a chance to get settled before you make them go to work. After that, a regular program of cutting back and heading will keep them in the desired shape and pay dividends.

Spraying

If you keep your trees well-pruned and clean, chances are the insects will pass them by. Insects are most likely to attack trees where they find weak or damaged wood. See to it that this is always removed immediately after an injury. Be sure to dispose of fruit-tree leaves in the fall. These leaves attract disease-bearing insects. Burn them in areas where burning is permitted.

Dormant-spray your trees in the late fall and early spring. Grandma said that, in her day, you sprayed fruit trees with nicotine sulphate mixed with two and a half pounds of laundry soap, like Fels-Naphtha, to fifty gallons of water. They fought red spiders with sour milk or buttermilk mixed with flour. Coddling moths on pears were fought by planting spearmint. I have learned that a dormant spray with a lime-sulphur solution and Volk oil combined sprayed on in the late fall when the foliage has dropped, and again in the spring before the buds swell does the job. This type of dormant spraying is especially effective if you give your fruit trees a good soap-and-water shampoo every month. If chemical control is necessary, use one of the many home-orchard sprays on the market *as directed*. It's a good idea to check with your ag-extension service for spraying times and sprays best suited to your local area. Make friends with these people . . . you help pay their salaries with your taxes.

With these few commonsense procedures your trees will be well protected and able to concentrate on their job of providing you and your family with mouth-watering tasties!

Whipping Your Tree

I am the guy who goes on television to tell Dinah Shore, Mike Douglas, and Johnny Carson to beat their trees. This always gets a few laughs . . . not to mention some raised eyebrows.

However, lots of people get the message and sneak out in the dead of night, when their neighbors are sleeping, to administer their tree whippings.

Whipping lazy fruit trees with a "bearing" switch is something I learned to do from Grandma Putt. It really works. Sometimes a tree suffers from "hardening of the arteries." Its sap vessels become constricted and don't carry the vital fluid to the leaves, buds, and spurs. Then, the tree's "metabolism" slows down and it is unable to bear fruit.

Use a three-to-four-foot sturdy willow switch and give your tree's trunk a thorough lacing as far as you can reach, and you will be amazed at the fruit that you will get old lazybones to produce.

What you are doing by spanking your tree is loosening the bark from the cadmium layer and stimulating circulation. Grandma said to whip your trees on moonlit nights in the early spring and you'll have a good harvest when bearing season arrives. Let neighbors arch their brows all they want . . . this works!

Nailing Up Bugs?

Another old-time orchardist's trick you may hear about, is nailing trees to get rid of caterpillars. That's right . . . nail your trees!

Old-timers used cast-iron nails and hammered them into their trees about a foot from the base, spacing them every four or five inches, according to the size of the tree. Folks who did this claimed that in a week or so all the caterpillars packed up and left the nailed trees, never to be heard from again.

According to the hammer-wielders, the iron in the nails oxidizes in the tree sap and turns to ammonia. The hint of ammonia evidently makes caterpillars gag. That's what this idea does to me, and if the trees could be interviewed on the subject, I'm sure their comment would be, "Ouch!"

Rub-A-Dub-Dub . . . Fruit Trees in a Tub

Yes, you can grow dwarf fruit trees in ceramic pots or wooden tubs. This is the only way you will have much chance of success at growing citrus fruit like oranges, lemons, and limes outside of southern California.

Keep increasing the size of the container every two years, to give the roots room to spread out. In four years or so, you should have placed your tree in its permanent home. For dwarf trees, the final tub size can be limited to 2 x 2 feet. You can keep your tree in this size tub if you prune it severely to a height of 3½ to 4 feet. It is also important to trim the roots back every two years, or whenever you repot. The final root ball should fit comfortably in the 2 x 2 foot tub. The tub should be placed on a castered platform so it can be wheeled indoors whenever chilly weather or frost threatens. These trees need lots of light in the spring and summer, but can take a dark basement or garage storage in the winter dormant period.

Your pots and tubs should have good drainage. You should water them regularly, but be careful not to overwater or the roots will rot. Feeding potted trees is only necessary in early spring and after they bear fruit in the fall. A handful of mild, balanced fertilizer is enough. Don't forget to dormant-spray these little fellows twice a year just as you would any other fruit trees.

These tub fruit trees can be lots of fun and will thrill you every now and again with a baby-bumper harvest.

Cold-Climate Varieties

People who live in parts of the country where there are cold winters, can grow the following fruits. Remember that apples and pears are often self-unfruitful . . . it takes two to tango!

With certain exceptions, I recommend dwarf or semi-dwarf fruit trees. These trees have proven themselves to be more efficient and practical for the modern homeowner and apartment gardener. Here are some recommended varieties for each type fruit:

Apples
Arkansas
Cortland
Earli Blaze
Golden Delicious
Starkrimson Delicious
Lodi
Red McIntosh
Winesap
Yellow Transparent
Rhode Island Greening

(I don't believe this variety comes in dwarf trees. If you like apple pies and have the room, it's worth making an exception.)

Apricots
Hungary
Blenheim
Erli-Orange
Farmingdale
Moongold
Royal

Crabapples
Dolgo Crab
Jacques
Rescue

Cherries
Sour: Northern Star
Sweet: Bing (self-unfruitful; plant another variety to cross-pollinate.)

Windsor

Nectarines
Lexington

Pocahontas
Stark Delicious

Peaches
Burbank
Elberta
Champion
Hale-Haven
Hal-Berta Giant
Golden Jubilee
Rio Oso Gem

Pears
Anjou
Bartlett
Chapp's Favorite
Seckel

Plums
Burbank
Damson
Green Gage
Golden Transparent Gage
South Dakota
Stanley

Quinces
Orange

Warm-Climate Varieties

Thousands of people are moving to California and Florida every week. Add to those the new residents in Hawaii, and you begin to realize that many new gardeners are curious about home-garden varieties of fruit native to those parts. Here are some that I can recommend:

Avocados
Anaheim   (California and Hawaii)
Bacon   (California and Hawaii)
Fuerte   (California and Hawaii)
Hass   (California and Hawaii)
Taylor   (Florida)

Bananas
Cavandish (Florida)
Lady Finger (Florida,
   Hawaii and other banana-raising areas)

Dates
Medjool   (Arizona and California)

Guavas
Varieties are available at local nurseries.

Kumquats
Marumi
Nazami

Mangoes
Haden
Kent
Pope

Olives
Manzanillo

Mission
Sevillano

Papayas
Varieties available at local nurseries.

Pineapples
Natal Queen
Smooth Cayenne

Pomegranates
Wonderful

Citrus Fruits
Most citrus fruits should be grown in California, the West Coast, Florida or a few areas in the Southwest. You can grow some in pots or tubs in other parts of the country.

Grapefruit
Marsh
Royal

Lemons
Eureka
Lisbon

Limes
Bearss
Persian

Mandarins and Tangerines
Dancy Tangerines
King Orange

Kinnow
Satsuma

Oranges
Hamlin
Plaquemines Sweet
Washington Navel
Temple
Valencia

Sour Oranges
Varieties available at local nurseries.

Tangelos
Minniola
Orlando

Chapter 8.
Nuts
in the Attic

For some mysterious, but wonderful, reason, the least ecology-minded real-estate developer can be counted on to avoid cutting down a stand of nut trees, or even a rare solitary specimen. These guys, who normally bulldoze everything in sight to squeeze out that last available square foot, seem to know that nut trees make land more valuable. And the homeowners who buy these trees along with the family homestead seem to have some obscure, or subconscious, understanding that "nuts are nice." Of course, any good amateur anthropological social psychologist (of whom there are many in my family) would most likely observe that people have been eating nuts as long as the squirrels have.

All this is my way of getting around to suggesting that you should treasure and use the nut trees you find growing on your property, and plant them where there are none so you and your family can harvest good crackin', pickin', and eatin'!

Varieties of Nuts

Americans have a rich and plentiful supply of native nuts to choose from when it comes to selecting trees and shrubs that will add beauty to their landscape and nuts to their attics.

Peanuts Are Nut-Peas

America's number one favorite nut is not a nut at all. Peanuts are actually legumous vegetables and could more properly be called "nut-peas." Now who in the world would want a nut-pea butter and jelly sandwich?

Peanuts grow best in the southern part of the country from the Atlantic as far west as Texas. But, they do best in the Southeast. My friend Ed Nelson, who raises children and avocados in California, is something of a nut expert having been raised both in peanut and pecan country. Ed, who makes a terrific pecan pie, once fed me some green Georgia boiled peanuts. I guess that is how those rebels separate the men from the carpetbaggers. Talk about "the green-apple quickstep" . . . green peanuts are a real pace-setter!

Ed says peanuts are classified as "bunchers" or "runners." Good varieties include Early Runner and Starr, but you can plant any shelled, unroasted kind you get at a health-food store. Grow them in a vegetable planting bed as you would peas or bush beans. Peanuts take about 3½ months to mature. Specific varieties may take longer. Grow them with popcorn so you can have a ball game in the fall.

Common Native North American Nuts

acorns	macadamia
beechnut	pignut hickory
black walnut	shellbark hickory

butternut	peanut
coconut	pecans
hazelnut	pine nuts

American chestnut . . . This great native tree was once the living centerpiece to many American town squares. In the early 1900s, the American chestnut was wiped out by a fungus disease. If you ever saw one of these magnificent trees, or know where a survivor still stands, count it as a treasure that can be shared by practically no one else in future years.

Foreign Imports Worth Growing and Eating

almond	heartnut
Carpathian walnut	filbert
cashew	ginkgo
Chinese chestnut	litchi (leechee)
English walnut	pistachio

Your Nut Tree Needs a Girl Friend

Don't think you will be able to tuck a nut tree or hazelnut shrub into some corner of your garden or home landscape. Nut trees grow big . . . very big! These are the kind of majestic giants you will want to consider as shade trees or large ornamentals on your property. The best example of what I mean is the black walnut. A mature black walnut will scrape the sky at 150 feet and it will have huge limbs that stretch outward and upward some thirty to fifty feet. So space is the single most important consideration.

Space is doubly important when you realize that some nut types are largely self-unfruitful. As you probably know by now, this means they will need *another* variety for cross-pollination purposes or they won't bear any nuts. Included in this group are almonds, butternuts, chestnuts, hazelnuts, hickories, macadamias, pecans, pistachios, black walnuts, and most English walnuts.

Buy two-year-old nursery stock, or take a tip from the squirrels and chipmunks and plant your own nuts in the fall. If you do this, plant them in damp, fertile soil and use window screening to keep those busy varmints away from your hoard. Water thoroughly in spring and summer. Mulch deeply and feed regularly except in bearing season. Nut trees don't need a lot of care, but when they start to bear pick up all the nuts and fallen debris and leaves you find under the tree. Store the nuts, burn or dispose of the leaves and debris.

In most cases, it takes several years before your nut crops are plentiful. This is just Mother Nature's way of getting you accustomed to her pace and schedule . . . but, it is no reason for you not to grow nuts!

Nutting

Ever since Americans left the farms and rural towns to create the urban sprawl, nuts have gone ungathered. In my book that is a crime against Mother Earth and Mother Nature . . . our natural godmothers.

Going nutting was another glorious adventure for me when I lived at Grandma Putt's. Fancy nut gatherers take a picnic basket, but most boys travel relatively unencumbered, with three or four old cloth cornmeal bags or gunny sacks.

It's best to spot your black walnut trees, butternuts, and shagbark (shell bark) hickories before you actually go nutting. Black walnuts are easiest to spot because they lose their leaves before any other tree in the woods or in country pastures. They grow from New Hampshire to mid-Nebraska, south to east Texas, and Alabama.

Butternuts grow wild all over the North from the middle of Maine to South Dakota and as far south as the northern part of Arkansas, Mississippi, and Georgia. Here, in Michigan, they even grow in the Upper Peninsula. Silhouetted against an autumn sky, they stand out like a big letter Y.

Shagbark hickories are easily recognizable from their bark that curls up in two-foot gray patches to make an obstacle course for overeager squirrels trying to harvest the tree's tasty nuts. This tree is a loner and a stand-out. Any boy who has even swung a Louisville Slugger knows hickory wood makes the best baseball bats! The largest hickory is the pecan. It grows from southern Wisconsin to Louisiana, all up and down the Mississippi Valley and over to mid-Texas, Oklahoma, and Kansas. The nut bushes stay on the tree well into winter.

Beech trees are beautiful. Their silver bark and yellow leaves are surely one of the reasons men become landscape artists.

Black walnuts are the tastiest nuts I know. Grandma said the Indians harvested them for centuries calling them round nuts. Jam the husks with the heel of your shoe to split them off. Be careful when you take the nuts out of the husks because they will stain your hands brown. As I write this I can almost smell them . . . their fragrance is one of the great American smells—and black walnut fudge is superb!

Butternuts are close relatives and are often called white walnuts. Grandma sometimes pickled them without drying them. The husks are sticky to the touch. After you de-husk them, soak a bag of them in a bucket of warm water, then hang the bag out on a clothesline to dry. (I wonder if anyone still has a clothesline? . . . If not, hang your bag on a nail somewhere.) This will make it easy to crack the thin shells without smashing the meat.

Hazelnuts are easiest to crack. The kernels are roundish and firm. They grow on tall shrubs in the East or in the Northwest on short trees. Sometimes they will fail to bear for several years, then suddenly you will reap a bumper crop.

Another great-tasting nut is the beechnut. You'll find it growing in the woods. The yellow leaves stay on well into winter, so wait 'til then. They are easy to pry out of their husks with your thumbnail, and are small-kerneled but sweet to the taste. Good-bearing beechnut trees are becoming harder and harder to find. Maybe it's the smog. If you have an extra handful to spare, send 'em my way.

White oak acorns used to be sweet and flaky, but everyone who has tried them lately says they're tough and bitter.

My nut friend, Ed Nelson, says that up in Wrightwood, California, where he has a cabin, pine nuts are gathered in profusion and sold at some roadside stands. I know this was an Indian staple, but I've never tried them. This just reminds me that I'll have to ask him to send me some.

Storing Your Hoard of Nuts

Deer and blue jays eat nuts, but the real nut experts are the squirrels. These playful varmints know enough to store the nuts they can't eat right away. You should copy their methods. Squirrels put their nuts away in the crotch of a protected nearby tree limb, or in some sandy soil. You will discover that too much moisture makes nuts lose their flavor or become rancid. Store in a cool, dry place like the squirrels. Black walnuts, particularly, are not too good fresh-gathered, but taste super after being stored in this way!

Grandma Putt kept her nuts stored up in the attic, where it was cool and dry during the winter. On wet, snowy days, when it wasn't fit for man or beast to go outside and tramp about, I would go up there with one of Grandma's big clay mixing bowls and fill it with handfuls of the black walnuts, hickory nuts, hazelnuts, and butternuts spread out over the floor to dry. Then I'd go down and sit in the big leather Morris chair by the side bay window and crack and pick nuts for hours watching the snow fall and listening to the wind howl.

My kids are so used to eating pistachio nuts, almonds, English walnuts, or peanuts from a can, that they've never learned how to use a nut pick. Cracking and picking nuts with a nut pick is a real challenge. At one time I was very proficient at this dying art form. To crack a hickory nut and pick out some large chunks of the kernel was so exacting an operation, that it was tempting not to eat the biggest one 'til you picked one even bigger.

Chestnutting

One late autumn evening the fire was crackling in the fireplace and we were all gathered around it "cracking" and "picking" away. Grandma said the noise of the burning logs reminded her of when she was a girl and Grandpa Putt was courting her. She said no wood spit and crackled like chestnut wood. Folks used to say the burning wood was complaining because you were roasting its nuts.

In those days one of the most anticipated fall activities was for a young man to take his gal chestnutting. Grandma said sometimes she and Grandpa would spend the greater part of the day strolling arm in arm all over the woods and meadows, looking for a likely tree. Since chestnut trees were enormous, they must have been concentrating more on each other than tree-hunting.

American chestnut trees were magnificent with enormous low-spreading limbs and gray-brown bark. The first sunny day after a fall frost was the time to gather chestnuts. The frost split open the large burrs that held the flavorful meaty nuts. Then it was easy to extract the chestnuts and fill a picnic basket or several bags from one tree. Grandma said Grandpa carved their names on a young chestnut tree they found once in Fowler's woods, and that one spring nearly forty years later, she could barely make out the faded letters on an old hollow log.

It's sad what happened to the American chestnut, but for folks who used to gather nuts on crisp fall days, they're still the number-one all-American nut. Maybe some of the nostalgia they create can be rekindled if you plant Chinese or Japanese chestnuts . . . but I rather doubt it.

Chapter 9.
Grandma's
Root Cellar

During the years of World War II, one of which I spent at Grandma Putt's, an estimated 63 million Americans were involved in raising home-grown fruits and vegetables as part of the Victory garden program. Food was rationed. Many of the most common kitchen staples, which had been available year-round before the war, were diverted to feed our army and navy and those of our allies. Consequently, it became necessary for folks to take up some of the age-old practices of their forefathers in order to store and preserve the foods they raised in their home gardens.

For Grandma this was nothing new. Storing food, canning, and preserving it was just a normal part of the annual fall and winter work. These were things that all people close to the earth had done for years. I believe that more and more people who are just now getting caught up in the pleasures and rewards of gardening, will go on to rediscover techniques and methods to help make the most efficient use of their harvests. Moreover, the proper autumn and wintering operations will make it possible to renew their partnership with Mother Nature on even stronger terms in the spring . . . providing even more plentiful, bountiful and beautiful results in the years to come.

A Good Place for Storing Vegetables and Fruit

One of the most vivid memories I have of Grandma's big old house is the cellar. There were two ways to get to it. The first, and least interesting, was through a kitchen door next to the pantry. This led down to the furnace and the big old washing machine. The best way to get into the cellar was through a stairway outside the house covered by a slanted double door. The stairs led down to the cellar. When the double door was closed, it was fun to slide down the outside of it. This was a short-lived summer and winter pastime, that lasted only as long as I couldn't think of anything better to do. The closed cellar stairway was also a good place to hide during evening games of hide-and-seek.

When the double doors were opened, the root cellar was bright, fragrant and inviting. Grandma kept it very clean. She said it was foolish to store clean food in a dirty cellar. Cleaning the cellar was an annual spring chore. Once she gave me a large paint brush and several gallons of whitewash and had me paint the entire storage area. Unfortunately, I wasn't as lucky as Tom Sawyer . . . no one happened by.

The Cold Cellar

This cold cellar, as Grandma called it, was divided into two rooms. The first was really not under the house at all, but used one side of the foundation as a wall. This was where she kept her potatoes, pumpkins, squash, cabbage-family members, and cold-packed jars of canned goods. Apples were stored here too, bushels and barrels of them! Their fragrance hung in the dark, cool air like an invisible perfume. Members of the cabbage family were wrapped in several thick layers of newspaper to prevent their "perfume" from escaping and flavoring the apples. (Be extra careful not to bruise pears or apples when you store them; this causes spoilage which can infect an entire barrel or bin. Place them in your cool storage area immediately after picking.)

Concrete walls and a dirt floor kept this part of the cold cellar moderately moist. It stayed cool here even in the summer, and going down to get a pickle was one of my favorite cooling-off tricks on a hot afternoon in July or August. Grandma insisted that I keep the doors shut tight to keep out hungry field mice.

The adjoining part of the cold cellar was a second storage room. This was situated entirely under the house. It had a concrete floor, two wooden walls, and was somewhat drier—but just as cool. Here Grandma stored dried beans, peas, and onions. The onions were up off the floor where the air could get at them. On the other side of a connecting door, in the furnace room, were two big double bins for sweet potatoes. This particular vegetable needs warm, dry air for proper storage.

The Root Cellar

Grandma's root cellar, as the name implies, was where she kept beets, radishes, parsnips, carrots, rutabagas, and turnips. It really wasn't a cellar at all, but an old converted cistern. During the winter, this area was just above freezing and very, very moist. If you don't happen to have a basement, you can convert part of your garage for storage of most crops, and you can store celery and members of the carrot and turnip family in the ground. The Department of Agriculture bulletins and your local library offer information for building these areas, and for wintering crops in small ground caches. One good idea is to store several types of vegetables together (except the cabbage family), so that when you open one small cache or trench, you'll find all you need without disturbing other buried vegetables. Cabbage can be wrapped in newspaper or celery covered with straw and stored outside in a converted sandbox or cold frame. Keep the sand moist and the sandbox covered with leaves and boards. Cabbage flavor actually improves this way. Potatoes should be kept up off the floor, preferably in slatted bins to allow the air to circulate around them.

An old refrigerator that is too unsightly for your kitchen may be fine to use in your garage for winter storing of vegetables that need cold temperatures.

Cabbages are always a problem. Probably the best thing to do is store them in trenches. Take off any bad outside leaves, wrap them in newspaper, and place them in the trench with their heads down. Cover the heads with straw or hay and chicken wire. Brussels sprouts can be stored the same way, but pick the whole plant and keep the buds on it.

Preserving Food

As any young girl who has just taken a beginner's course in home economics will tell you, basic food preservation includes: freezing, canning, salting, pickling, and dehydrating or drying. Your garden products can be kept for months using one or more of these methods and following a few commonsense rules.

Vegetables good for freezing include broccoli (either freeze or eat fresh), corn, string beans, spinach, and all those you find frozen in supermarkets. I personally dislike frozen potatoes, but suit yourself. Once you get the hand of blanching and freezing fresh-picked crops, yours will taste better than any put out by the big food companies.

There has been a great revival in home canning in recent years. With the exception of cabbage, you can can anything from apricots to zucchini. Whether vegetables and fruits taste better canned or frozen is a matter that I will have to leave to your individual taste.

Grandma used to can with Ball and Kerr mason jars. Ilene, who uses Kerr jars and tops, says that these products have been improved measurably since Grandma's day. Now you can take the screw bands off after the jars have cooled and the seal is made. Don't use the lids more than once. Puncture the lid when you open a jar to avoid the temptation to use it a second time.

Here is a list put out by the Department of Agriculture which will give you an idea of how many quarts of food you can expect from an average bushel or crate of different garden products.

Approximate Yields

Legal weight of a bushel of fruits or vegetables varies in different states. These are average weights:

Food	Fresh	Canned
Apples	1 bu. (48 lb.)	16 to 20 qt.
Apricots	1 bu. (50 lb.)	20 to 24 qt.
Berries, except strawberries	24-qt. crate	12 to 18 qt.
Cherries, as picked	1 bu. (56 lb.)	22 to 32 qt.
Peaches	1 bu. (48 lb.)	18 to 24 qt.

Pears	1 bu. (50 lb.)	20 to 25 qt.
Plums	1 bu. (56 lb.)	24 to 30 qt.
Strawberries	24-qt. crate	12 to 16 qt.
Tomatoes	1 bu. (53 lb.)	15 to 20 qt.
Asparagus	1 bu. (45 lb.)	11 qt.
Beans, lima, in pods	1 bu. (32 lb.)	6 to 8 qt.
Beans, snap	1 bu. (30 lb.)	15 to 20 qt.
Beets, without tops	1 bu. (52 lb.)	17 to 20 qt.
Carrots, without tops	1 bu. (50 lb.)	16 to 20 qt.
Corn, sweet, in husks	1 bu. (35 lb.)	8 to 9 qt.
Okra	1 bu. (26 lb.)	17 qt.
Peas, green, in pods	1 bu. (30 lb.)	12 to 15 qt.
Pumpkin	50 lb.	15 qt.
Spinach	1 bu. (18 lb.)	6 to 9 qt.
Squash, summer	1 bu. (40 lb.)	16 to 20 qt.
Sweet potatoes	1 bu. (55 lb.)	18 to 22 qt.

(Above table reprinted from *United States Department of Agriculture Bulletin AIS-64.*)

Freezing and canning methods are explained simply and thoroughly in the *Kerr Home Canning* book which costs 35 cents. The company is located in Sand Springs, Oklahoma. If you don't want to spend 35 cents, but still want to can, consult your local library or the ag-extension service for bulletins and other information.

CAUTION: Certain bacteria can grow in a sealed jar if not destroyed by heat. Be careful whenever you process food to take every possible precaution. Be sure you know what you're doing and follow directions exactly.

Drying Garden Foods

You can dry apples, shell beans, limas, carrots, cherries, corn, currants, peppers, pumpkins, tomatoes, and other fruits and garden foods.

We would let the shell beans, limas, and peas dry on the vine. Grandma and Aunt Jane would sit around in the kitchen after supper shelling them for hours. The shelled seeds were dried in cloth bags until they became quite hard. Then the bag was pounded to break off the hard coating or hulls. Finally, they were cleaned in big crocks or basins of water. When all the hull-chaff was removed, the split peas or beans were stored in the dry part of the cold cellar with a packet of bug-repellent herbs in each tin, bag, or keg.

Grandma said that one reason we call snap beans "string" beans, is because pioneers used to string them up to dry from the rafters of their log cabins.

Dried herbs can be stored with the onions and shell beans, but Grandma kept hers mostly in the pantry.

Sauerkraut was made in a big ten gallon clay crock which was covered with a cloth and a plate. Every day, Grandma would take off the cloth to remove the scum at the top of the crock. Then, she would put on a clean cloth. This process was repeated until the kraut was cured. It took about a week and a half for the fermentation to be finished.

Wintering Flowers and Other Autumn Garden Tasks

At the end of September or in the early part of October, before the first frost, Grandma would dig around some of her geraniums, herbs, and other plants she intended to take inside for winter. Tender bulbs like dahlias and glads were brought to the cold cellar for storage.

To "take in and winter" geraniums, jerk them up by the roots when they turn brownish after the first frost. Lay each geranium kitty-corner on a double spread of newspaper and wrap it up. Put your wrapped up roots in a cool, damp basement and leave them there until March.

After March 15th, take your geraniums out and unwrap them. Cut off 1/3 of the roots, and 2/3 of the tops. Repot in clay pots filled with a mixture of half sand and half soil. To sterilize this soil, put it in a cake tin and place a potato on top. Now, roast at 250° until the potato is tender. At this stage of the operation, your soil is ready for planting in and your potato is ready for eating!

Potting Your Outside Plants

Grandma would use her trowel or a knife to cut a circle around the plants which she planned to put in pots. The circle was as round and as deep as the pot each plant was to go in. Instead of digging them out right away though, she would leave them cut out like that in the ground. This gave her pot plants a chance to absorb the initial shock of being cut up and moved. She watered them thoroughly and left them long enough for new rootlets to form within the ball. After about three and a half weeks, she lifted the new ball carefully out of the ground and placed it in its new pot home, where it was as happy and contented as if it had always lived there.

A modern version of this would be to use a thoroughly clean plastic bleach bottle with the top and bottom cut off. Force this down into the soil around your plant to help it reform its roots. After three and a half weeks, remove the plant in the plastic container. Repot and take inside.

Asparagus beds, brambleberries, roses, cherry, and peach trees, were heavily mulched with leaves and corn husks to prevent frost damage. All except the winter hardy grape vines were loosened from the trellis, pruned, laid down on the ground and covered with a heavy leaf mulch.

Winter pruning of fruit and nut trees helped create a kindling and firewood supply.

School in the country started later than in town because the boys were needed to work until the harvests were all completed. But, before long, we were into the fall and winter term and, except for after-school and weekend chores, the garden was allowed its winter sleep.

Winter was a time for tramping in the snow or sitting by the fire. The only gardening tasks were reading seed catalogues and harvesting a Christmas tree in the woods. When we brought the tree home, Grandma had me pot it in a bucket of half sand and half water. All the time it was in the house, she kept this bucket filled and she also kept a kettle of water boiling in the fireplace to add moisture to the room.

In recent years I have discovered an even more modern and successful method to help make your Christmas tree last and last. This is it:

Directions for Christmas-Tree Care

1. When you bring your tree home, cut off the end again as it has probably been damaged at the lot where you purchased it.

2. Stand tree in a stand or container that holds water.

3. Into one gallon of very hot water pour:
>   2 cups of clear corn syrup
>   4 tsps. old-fashioned bleach
>   4 tbsps. Greenguard Micronized Iron

4. Pour this solution into the tree stand or container.

5. Keep adding warm water every day until you take down the tree.

6. Use old tree for bird shelter in winter. Break it up for compost heap in the spring.

Then, in late winter, we would tap the maple sugar trees!!!

Making Maple Syrup and Maple Sugar

Maple syrup is one of the few crops produced only in North America, and was made by the Indians before the arrival of white settlers. You can use any kind of maple trees to tap for maple syrup, but sugar maples make the very best. Each tree should give about 4-6 pounds of sugar. You can make six pounds of sugar from twenty gallons of sap. Making either product is easy, here's how:

1. Pick a nice winter morning in late February or very early March. The exact timing depends on your local weather conditions. The snows should have begun to melt and best tapping days are after a frost the previous night.

2. Use a 1-inch auger bit to drill your first tap two inches into the tree. Never use an ax to cut channels in your tree. Two taps per tree are plenty. Insert a hollow wooden trough

or plastic tube that's been cut in half to collect the sap. Elder makes good troughs because the twigs and branches are hollow and the pith is easily removed to make a nice channel. It's strong enough to hold a hanging bucket. After a week or ten days, remove the tap and bore two inches deeper.

3. You can empty your sap buckets into a large container and carry it home or, if you want to avoid trekking back and forth, build a fire in an open spot in the woods. (Might be a good idea to check with the local fire department first, to make sure that's okay.) The fire will keep you warm while you're working. I usually end up going home at sundown and continue my boiling-down there. Check your buckets every day for more sap. It will take many, many hours to boil away the water to make maple syrup that's not terribly runny. And, many, many, many more hours to boil the syrup down into sugar.

4. For your syrup making, use a heavy-duty iron kettle. Scour it out with vinegar and sand before using. Don't use scouring powder.

5. Add about an ounce of pure limewater to every gallon of sap. The limewater neutralizes the sap and helps the sugar to granulate.

6. To make pure white sugar, take the brown "salts" resulting from step 5 and dissolve them in alcohol. Do it in this manner: Make several large cones out of galvanized sheet metal or hard plastic with an aperture at the small end. (These can be purchased from maple-syrup farms.) Put your brown sugar into the cones. Stop up the hole in the bottom until it is completely cool. Next, remove the stopper and pour rum or whisky into the base of the cone. Allow this to

245

filtrate through the opening until the sugar is white. Put the white sugar back in the cone to harden. Finally, take the white loaf of sugar from the cone, dissolve it in water to boil off the alcohol and allow to dry.

Waiting for Spring

These were just a few of the things to do at Grandma Putt's while I waited around for spring to come.

Chapter 10.
Spring
is a Good Time to
Talk to Flowers

I'm sure that many of us could live quite contentedly with far less than our present share of certain kinds of Mother Nature's bounties. Ilene, for instance, tells me every summer that she wishes that there were no mosquitos in Michigan. Some people in the West and South grow bored with all the nice weather in those parts and head out for snow country. Here in the North, my neighbor is fed up with his allotment of slush and blizzards and follows the birds to Florida. As the pastry jingle proclaims, "Everybody doesn't like *something* . . ." And, I suppose, there are even some people who would like to live far, far away from the flower fields that surround their homes. A world of plants without flowers might be a pleasant place for hay-fever sufferers. The simple fact is, that there are plenty of plants that live, prosper, reproduce, and die without ever bearing a single bloom. It's perfectly clear that God didn't *need* to make flowers. But I wonder what kind of a face Mother Earth would have without them?

What Good Are Flowers?

There is no accounting for taste, or regulating it. We flower lovers can't force scoffers to love or even like them. Many a self-satisfied vegetable gardener laughs up his sleeve at folks who grow only flowers.

"What are flowers good for?" he asks, as he munches an ear of hot-roasted buttered corn or crunches down on a fresh-pulled carrot. "You'd better pick the flowers off your potato plants if you want a good crop."

Herb growers find beauty in the leafy foliage of their parsley and in the fragrance of their purple-leaved sage. Fruit and nut men say you can get all the blossoms you need without ever planting a flower bed. Certain Japanese gardens I have seen are masterpieces of serenity and repose using only a quiet stream, some rocks, and a scattering of green plants. Everyone with a scientific nature, can see the beauty of a mathematical formula, but I believe it takes someone with the eye and spirit of an artist to see the truth and beauty reflected in the face of a flower. Grandma Putt said that we should all thank the Lord not only for creating the millions of flower varieties that cover the earth, but for letting so many of us feel the *need* to grow some of them in flower gardens. While I may not be able to defend the logic of that statement, I do follow her advice.

Communicate With Love

Grandma was years ahead of today's flower children with their message of love. She said that to grow flowers or any plants successfully, you have to love them and communicate your feelings to them. She spoke to them affectionately whenever she worked among them or walked in her garden. From the kind of results she got, it was obvious they responded positively to tender-loving-talk and tender-loving-care. She held that if you grow flowers, talk to them, and spend enough time in their company, you are bound to lose your ornery nature. She said you can learn an awful lot talking to your flowers on a nice spring morning. I think she was right because whenever I weed a flower bed I lose my grouchiness and start to smile. The smiles usually last all day.

Many a gardener I have met on my travels around the country, speaks with pride about talking to his plants and flowers. As often as not, he'll have a photograph or an outstanding specimen to prove that "communicating while you are cultivating" works wonders! If you don't believe me, why don't you try it? You've got nothing to lose and a whole lot to gain.

Since You Don't Have to Grow Flowers, Why Not Make it Easy on Yourself?

Grandma was never one to waste space and never one to make a nice job too hard. She said that since no one will ever force you to plant a flower bed you shouldn't plant one that's so large you have to work hard weeding it. All her flower beds that were against the house, hedges or fences were always 3 x 10 feet wide and long. The reason for making them no wider than 3 feet is because a hoe reaches 5½ feet. Those wide beds that are recommended so much in gardening books will make you stoop too much.

Wider flower beds will give you a better flow of continuous color than narrow beds. If that's what you want, plant your eight to ten foot wide beds in the open so you can work on them from either side. Or, if you want even bigger beds and have the space, incorporate a garden walk to help you get at the weeds more easily. The new preemergent weed killers can help you out with this chore too. Don't put them on 'til all your seedlings are up.

She also avoided sharp corners to her beds and made sure to set lawn border flowers back far enough to allow the lawn mower to trim the edge of the turf without snipping or trampling them.

Informal vs Formal Plantings

Like an artist who is going to paint a picture, I suggest you make a few preliminary sketches until you get the shape of your flower beds, their colors and flower placement just right. Decide whether you want to have free-flowing lines and natural-looking plantings, or the more traditional flower gardens of our ancestors. Proponents of either type have good arguments, so pick whichever suits your taste. Also, let the setting of your home and property and the type of flowers you intend to use guide you in making your decision. For instance, if you live near a woods and want to use some of the local wild flowers in your garden, it might be best to go "natural" and informal. Wildflowers have a way of being uncomfortable and unruly in formal layouts, kind of like the Beverly Hillbillies. Wildflowers also have subtle colors which are shown off better by soft curving lines than by abrupt straight borders. To lay out your informal beds use an old clothesline, long electrical extension cord or your garden hose. That way, you can get the curves just right before you begin to dig.

Formal beds often work best against walls, fences and hedges. Remember to use your sketch pad to design these too. Be sure to place the tallest flowers like hollyhocks, hardy asters, day lillies, gladioli, lupines, oriental poppies, phlox, peonies, snapdragons, and dahlias in the background so they won't block their shorter cousins from view or from the sunshine. If you intend a semiformal plantation, bring one of these tall guys up front every so often to break the monotony.

Like a lot of flowers that fell out of fashion, hollyhocks are coming back. When I was a kid, girls used to make dolls out of these flowers. They would turn the face of the flower upside down to make the skirt, stick a wire or toothpick through the center to make the body, use a second kind of flower to make a face and a third to make the bonnet.

In front of the "tall guys," plant flowers like heleniums, delphiniums, chrysanthemums, and daffodils.

Another flower that's regaining some of its lost esteem is the calceolara, or, grandma's pocketbook so called because the flowers are shaped like bright pouches. These come in several colors and grow well outside or indoors in pots in light soil or partial shade. When the flowers begin to wilt and turn color, pinch them off and new blooms will appear. Repot them, and return them to a north windowsill in the house before the frost.

Closer to the foreground, put in baby's breath, columbines, shasta daisies, gallardia, tulips, phlox, veronica, salvia, poppies, and zinnias.

For the front edging, you can plant low-growers like hardy alyssum, petunias, candytuft, crocus, pinks, chives, sedum, sundrops, lavender, verbena, dwarf tulips, and marigolds.

Obviously there are plenty of varieties to choose from, as this is a very sketchy list.

Plant the "tough guys," stronger flowers, like iris, at the ends of your beds. Kids are always running near the flowers and never seem to be able to make the corners. Iris will stand up again after a little close corner-cutting. Hen and chicken is another good corner plant.

Integration or Segregation?

Some flowers, like tulips and daffodils, do exceptionally well in large massed plantings. Daffodils are particularly popular because they grow so well in almost every climatic condition in this country. Some people I know, grow no other flowers. When making mass plantings of any type of flowers, you can limit your space to one color or a blending of several related colors. If you like tutti-frutti ice cream you may want to mix up your mass plantings the same way and have every color in the rainbow.

In Grandma's day, all the flowers were mixed in together, bulbs, biennials, annuals and perennials. She remembered or wrote down where everything was and when it was due to come up, so that none of her flower friends ever got in each other's way. In recent years, the single-type mass plantings have been the rule of fashion for flower gardens. As far as I'm concerned, it never hurts to mix up your flower charges. Getting them gossiping and growing together will be more eye-pleasing and delightful than you might at first imagine.

Pass the Paint Brush

Plan your colors so that they blend together in a harmonious way that appeals to you and seems to go with your setting. Consider the foliage of plants that bloom for only a short time. Don't let those with rough or drab foliage have a conspicuous place. You can plan for your colors to remain the same, or change dramatically, with the seasons.

Use your child's crayons or paint set to color your sketch. This will let you see if you are planning the right color blendings. If the total effect on paper isn't pleasing, tear up the sketch and begin studying your catalogues again.

Take Your Climate into Consideration

When you plant your flower gardens, be sure to take your local climate and weather into consideration. Last year, more than 36 million Americans moved to a new place of residence. Many of these went to different states. If you are among them, don't just assume that the flowers you grew in the East will grow in the West, or that northern-temperate-zone varieties will thrive in the humid or tropical South. around the new neighborhood for the best gardens. Introduce yourself. You'll be surprised how willing, able, and eager old-timers are to give newcomers like you their sage advice and the benefit of their experience and mistakes.

Altitude

Certain plants which, at first glance, might seem to be suited to a tropical climate, may do very well in most parts of this country. A good example of this is the tuberous begonia family. Although these begonias originated in an equatorial country, Bolivia, they grow very well in the temperate north. The reason for this is that Bolivia is extremely mountainous with elevations up to 15,000 feet or more. The higher plants grow, the more cold-hardy they will be. Westerners who buy mountain cabins in ski country can use these new locations to grow northern flower varieties. The local ag-extension office and year-round residents can also help you choose plants for these new growing climates.

Flowering Trees and Shrubs

When planning your flower gardens, don't overlook certain flowering trees and shrubs to be used as focal points to blend with the flowers in certain parts of your landscape. Among these are: almonds, apples, cherries, crabs, dogwoods, lemons, lilacs, hawthorns, magnolias, oranges, peaches, plums, quinces, rose trees, tulip trees, viburnum, and weigela (a shrub of the honeysuckle family).

Don't overlook colorful nonflowering trees like the sunburst locust, pin oak, and red maple, to provide flower-garden backgrounds.

Flowering Vines and Hedges

In addition to members of the rose family, there are many varieties of vines and hedges you will want to consider including in the total picture that represents your flower gardens. Among the most popular vines are black-eyed Susan, bougainvillea, clematis, hydrangea, honeysuckle, mock orange, morning glory, pyrancantha, sweet pea, and the beautiful wisterias. These flowering vines can add a hanging dimension of color or a background which blends with the flowers growing below them.

A background of single-colored or green foliaged hedge will help your bright flowers ping out. Here are a few of the most common: Alpine currant, amur privet, buckthorn, Chinese lilac, dwarf cranberry bush, dwarf holly, dwarf nine-back, dwarf winged eunonymus, forsythia, Froebel spirea, Korean boxwood, privet, weeping hemlock.

American Flowers

Flowers have been brought to this continent, and are under cultivation and development here, from every corner of the world. China, Turkey, Russia, Greece, Italy, Bulgaria and northern Europe are the original sources of many of the common flowers you will want to grow in your garden today. But even if you ignored all these commonly cultivated old-world flowers, you could still plant an enormous spectrum of rainbow-hued varieties—enough to please even the most extreme shape, size, and color cravings.

Among the best-known and most frequently grown flowers that originated in the western hemisphere are purple aster, begonia, bougainvillea, cactus, California poppy, canna, cleome, columbine, coral bells, dahlia, Tahoka daisy, dogwood, frangipani, fuschia, gaillardia, glory bush, gloxinia, heliotrope, dwarf iris, copper iris, crested iris, jack-in-the-pulpit, jacobinia, jewelweed, American laurel, mountain laurel, lemon vine, fairy lilly, trout lily, zephyr lily, lupine, magnolia, marigold, meadow rue, milkweed, mountain rose, nasturtium, nicotiana, orchid, oxalis, pachysandra, passion-flower, pentstemon, petunia, perskia, phlox, poinsettia, Mexican tulip poppy, prettyface, native rhododendrums, rose moss, Russellia, blue sage, scarlet sage, blue salvia, scarlet salvia, pink silene, slipperflower, slipperplant, black snake-root, Solomon's seal, spider flower, Virginia spiderwort, stigmaphyllon, sunflower, sun-rose, sweet shrub, tabebuia, tickseed, touch-me-not, trillium, verbena, yucca and zinnia.

This impressive, but only partial, list is continually being enlarged with the addition of newly discovered tropical species and newly developed American hybrids of old-world flowers.

Plan for the Seasons

From the last days of winter to the last days of autumn, your flowers will bloom in five major waves or tides of color. These are the late winter and early spring bloomers; mid-spring bloomers; early summer bloomers; mid-summer bloomers; and fall to early winter bloomers. With only a few exceptions in the South and Southwest, your flowers can be put into one of these easy-to-remember categories. Of course you can move your blooming times up or back by winter-forcing and succession planting.

To keep a constant flow of color and to take full advantage of each of the five blooming periods, you will have to include bulbs, perennials, annuals, and biennials in your planting and planning.

Bulbs

Tubers, corms, and true bulbs make up what we gardeners commonly call the "bulb family." Don't spend too much time worrying about the differences between the three types since they are generally planted and cared for in the same way. This lovable flower family will help make your garden bloom for all except the coldest months of the year.

Luckily for us, Mother Nature and the nurseryman have combined to sort out the bulb stock for us. The convenient result of this sorting will give you three main groups, which are easy to get to know and care for. They are: hardy, spring and summer flowering bulbs; the half-hardy summer flowering bulbs and the tender, summer or autumn flowering bulbs.

HARDY SPRING AND SUMMER FLOWERING BULBS

These are the bulbs you will find available for sale in the late summer. Hardy bulbs in this group should be planted in the fall and are hardy enough to stay in the ground over the freezing winter months. Among the hardy bulb varieties are small bulbs which put in the earliest appearance of any flowers, and the large bulbs (many of these are the famous Dutch bulbs). They are obviously also divided as spring bloomers and summer bloomers.

DUTCH BULBS

The hardy bulbs are usually referred to as Dutch bulbs. But if you come from the Balkans, Turkey, southern Russia or Afghanistan, you have every right to think of them as part of your own natural heritage. The lilies Solomon saw, were probably the red lily, common to Syria and Judea. Roses and lilies were brought to the West by way of Greece, and, much later, by the conquering Arabs by way of North Africa and Spain.

The "Dutch" bulbous iris (and other rhizome iris varieties), grew wild in eastern Asia before recorded history, and was early developed by the Japanese, but scientists and plant historians believe it is native as far east and north as China, west to central Europe and from India to North Africa. For many of the ancient peoples who lived in those areas, the iris became a symbol of great religious significance.

Tulips come from Turkey and parts east of there. The Austrian ambassador to the Ottoman Empire saw fields of tulips when he was stationed there in 1554. He purchased some for his garden back home. During the next eighty years, Europe went tulip crazy!

Holland became a center for selling tulips and other hardy bulb stock. The prices realized on tulip futures would bug out the eyes of today's big butter-and-egg men! A single new type could make a man extremely wealthy. Then, in 1636, the bottom fell out of the Dutch bulb business. It was like our own 1929 stock-market crash. Important Dutchmen woke up one day to find themselves flat broke. It took more than three hundred years for Dutch bulbs to regain the same kind of popularity in Europe. By the beginning of WW II, tulips were once again Europe's number one sought-after flower. Dutch bulbs were being exported all over the world. Since the big storms that hit the Netherlands after WW II, Dutch bulb imports to the United States have dropped to a trickle compared to the 100,000,000 we purchased in 1940. But the market for these hardy bulbs, grown now in the northwest coastal states, Virginia, and right here in Holland, Michigan, is growing every year.

THE LITTLE FELLERS

The smallest hardy bulbs bloom before Old Man Winter has ended his annual visit. They are the tell-tale sign that he is just about ready to start packing. Like the tulips, these "little fellers" are best planted in the late fall and on into the winter. They include crocus, glory-of-the-snow (chionodoxa), snowdrop, winter aconite, and the scillas.

THE BIG GUYS

The large hardy bulbs include lilies, iris reticulata (Dutch iris), hyacinths, daffodils (narcissus family), and tulips. Lilies and hyacinths should be planted in the late summer or early fall. Tulips, iris, and daffodils can be planted later (at the same time as the little fellers above). If you plant them after the first frost, use planting mix and mulch with compost or leaves to keep the soil temperature around them as constant as possible. Freezing won't harm them, but alternate thawing and freezing all winter long, will.

THE HARDY SUMMER AND AUTUMN FLOWERING BULBS

Most summer flowering bulbs stand up tall to be counted. Included among these are: lilies in variety (my favorite is the regal, but Easter lilies can be set out in the garden and tiger lilies are the easiest to grow. Consult a lily man or one of the fine books on this flower's culture). Also, summer hyacinths and hardy amaryllis should be included in this group.

Shorter-stemmed members of this group are: saffron flower (colchium), hardy cyclamen, and autumn crocus. If you live in the extreme north, mulch the least hardy of these to give winter temperature protection.

THE HALF-HARDY, SUMMER FLOWERING BULBS

These include calla lilies, montbretias, spider lilies, and hardy begonias. In many parts of the country, these can be left in the ground through the winter. I wouldn't advise this though if you live north of the Ohio river.

THE TENDER SUMMER AND FALL FLOWERING BULBS

To me, these are the bulbs that really make bulb-growing worth while. Don't be misled by gardening books into believing that these tender darlings are too much trouble and have to be coddled. Don't you join the ranks of those ostrich-heads who miss out on growing their own dahlias, cannas, tuberous begonias, gladioli, tuberoses, anemones, and caladiums.

Baker's List of Bulb-Planting and Culture Tips

1. You can start to grow bulbs like tulips, hyacinths, daffodils, etc., indoors, or in pots wrapped with newspaper and buried under the ground for 8-10 weeks. This will give you winter pot-plant beauty and fragrance as well as an early start for middle and late spring bloomers.

2. Plant the earliest bloomers, like winter aconite, crocus, snowdrop, scilla (Siberian squill, etc.), in clumps as soon as they are available in snow country and in early December in

the south and west. Best planting depth is about 3 inches. These plants unfold their tender little blossoms from February through March. Snowdrops and crocuses like sunny exposure if you want them to open at the earliest possible date. The others, can take partial shade and damp soil. Mulch until they bloom, then remove the mulch but keep the soil moist.

3. Lilies should be set out in the early fall, the earlier the better. Plant about 8-10 inches deep and 15-20 inches apart. Lilies are often planted in groups. Their planting bed should be of well-drained soil. Cold-storage lilies are also available for wintering inside. Check with your nurseryman.

4. Most of the true bulbs, like tulips, develop deep root systems. Plant them as soon as the weather cools in early winter until the ground freezes. Plant hyacinths, daffodils, and tulips six inches deep and six inches apart. Don't plant them in the same soil where they grew last year without refortifying it.

5. For mass plantings or large plantings of several types, dig up the entire bed to 8 inches. Remove the soil and improve it by mixing in two pounds of bone meal, five pounds of gypsum and about ten pounds of peat moss for each bushel of garden soil. Refill the bed with this planting mixture.

6. Plant the deepest bulbs on the bottom, with the tops up. Don't plant your bulbs upside down. Cover them with soil. Next, lay in the second layer. Be sure not to plant these right on top of the first layer. The small bulbs, or daffodils can be planted in clusters as they look best growing in attractive clumps. As you finish with each layer, continue in a like manner on the next one, up until you are finished. Don't

plant too shallow. Late bulbs should be the deepest, early bloomers on the top layer. Careful planning should give you two months of flowers.

7. Now, mulch the top with leaves, light bark, pine needles or wood chips. This will protect your bulbs from temperature fluctuations during the winter.

8. As soon as there are signs that your bulbs are ready to emerge, remove the mulch and feed with a handful of 4-12-4 or 5-10-5 garden food. Feed before they bloom. This will help them become strong and bloom longer.

9. A soap-and-water shampoo is a body-booster for your young bulbs. Apply this before your blooms appear.

10. After blooming, check your bulbs for insect damage. If any is present, dust the *soil* with 10 percent chlordane.

11. As blooms fade, pick off the seed pods and wait as long as you can before you cut off the stems. Hyacinths, daffodils, tulips, etc., need healthy stems to help fatten up the bulb for next year. When the foliage turns yellow, bend it down and fasten in a tight ball with a rubber band. Wait until all the tulip foliage has dried up, then cut it off just above ground level.

12. If you decide to dig up your hardy bulbs in order to divide or move them, do this just when the foliage dies. In this case, don't cut the foliage off. I always try to break them apart and replant them right away, but it is all right to cold-store them like onions.

13. Plant *tender* bulb stock like: tuberous begonias, cannas, gladioli, tuberose, etc., as soon as the ground warms up. Prepare the bed as with tulips. Tuberous begonias like north exposure, half sun, half shade. They need lots of moisture and slightly acid soil. Use a pine needle mulch. Dahlias are my favorite summer bulbs. The blooms can be enormous. They like almost any type of soil, but I plant mine in sandy loam that's well drained. Start your dahlias indoors in pots and move them outside as soon as the ground gets warm. Plant four inches deep. You can ignore some of the garden book rules. The books say to nip off extra buds and grow one flower per plant. I do this part of the time (when I want big single blooms) but I sometimes just let my dahlias grow the way Mother Nature intended.

If you want glads (gladioli) all summer long, make succession plantings. Plant them in your bed a half foot deep and every two weeks, from the beginning of warm soil in April until the Fourth of July. As with tulips, wait until the foliage dries before digging the bulbs out for winter storage. Dry-store them in the same place as onions.

Here is a list of best-loved bulbs according to the approximate order of their appearance in late winter to late autumn. You'll have to adjust according to your local growing conditions and climate to determine the blooming dates for your area.

Late Winter—
Early Spring
snowdrop
spring crocus
winter aconite
scillas (Siberian
   squill, etc.)

glory-in-the-snow
  (chionodoxa)
anemone blanda
triteleias
Puskinia libanotica
iris reticulata
early tulips (clusiana)

fosteriana
grape hyacinth
hardy orchid
trumpet daffodil
single and double
    early tulips
short daffodils
poets' narcissus
jonquils

Mid-Spring
late tulips
biflora tulips
parrot tulips
cottage tulips
lily-flowered tulips
double late tulips
Darwin tulips
late bloom hyacinths
breeder tulips
late bloom narcissus
peony flowered tulips

Late Spring—
Early Summer
caladiums
calla lilies
gladioli
freesias
crocosmia
hardy begonia
climbing lily

cannas
buttercup (ranunculus)

Mid-Summer—
Early Autumn
tigridia
spider lily
amaryllis
aster lily
dahlia (all types)
harlequin lily
montbretia
tuberous begonia
tuberose

Autumn—
Early Winter
autumn flowering
    hardy amaryllis
cape hyacinth
camellia begonia
rose begonia
carnation begonia
climbing lily
cyclamen
colchicum
    (saffron flower)
autumn crocus

House-Plant Bulbs

In addition to individuals from the above list, the following varieties make excellent bulbs to grow indoors.

agapanthus
achimenes
amarcrinum
amaryllis hippeastrum
scarborough lily

gloxinia
nerine
chinchincheree
freesia

The Soil and the Location of Your Flower Beds

No matter how dry, moist or poor the soil conditions of your future flower bed may be, I'm willing to bet you can talk some varieties of the flowers listed below to grow and thrive there. (A-annual; P-perennial)

Flowers for Dry Soil		
A	blue sage	
A	California poppy	
A	cleome	
A	cornflower	
A	four-o'clock	
A	gaillardia	
A	portulaca	
A	scarlet sage	
A	star-of-Texas	
A	sunflower	
A	zinnia	
P	baby's breath	
P	betony	
P	sunflower	
P	bearded trees	

P catmint
P evening primrose
P coneflower
P catchfly
P yucca
P hardy aster

Flowers for Moist Soil
A forget-me-not
A begonia
A calendula
A impatiens
A mallow
A monkey flower
A nicotiana

A	phlox	A	gaillardia
A	sweet pea	A	marigold
P	geum	A	morning glory
P	columbine	A	nasturtium
P	trollius	A	portulaca
P	forget-me-not	A	sweet alyssum
		A	zinnia
		P	coneflower
Flowers for Poor Soil		P	dianthus
A	California poppy	P	bearded iris
A	cleome	P	snowball
A	four-o'clock	P	sunflower

However, most flowers flourish in good sandy loam . . . prepare it as you would for a vegetable or herb garden and watch them smile!

Remember, perennials are deeper rooted than annuals . . . work your perennial beds as deeply as possible before planting. Add plenty of well-rotted cow manure or compost.

Shade-Tolerant Flowers

Everywhere I go, someone says, "Mr. Baker, I have this peculiar problem . . ." As soon as I hear that opening phrase, I can almost guess what will follow. . . . ". . . a great deal of my garden is in shade. What flowers will I be able to grow in those shady spots?" Well, don't despair, my friends. Mother Nature took shady spots into consideration when she began selecting flowers. Here are just a *few* shade tolerant varieties:

Perennials
anemone
bleeding heart
columbine

coral bells
aster
foxglove
day lily

iris
peony
evening primrose
lily of the valley
forget-me-not
primrose
violet

balsam
cleome
China aster
larkspur
petunia
snapdragon
stock
verbena

Annuals
amaranthus

Flowers for Cutting

Grandma Putt kept her cut-flower plantings tucked away in various nooks and corners, and a fairly large bed out near the vegetable garden, where it wouldn't be so noticeable after a recent reaping. She cut some flowers for beauty, others for their fragrance, and still others from thinnings.

Here is a partial list of some easy-to-grow flowers for cutting and using for arrangements inside:

For Beauty

anthemis moonlight
day lily
wallflower
sweet pea
roses
daffodils
phlox
chrysanthemum
tulip
dahlia
stock
baby's breath

foxglove
peony
Canterbury bells
lilies of the valley
lilacs
pansy
petunia
yarrow
Helen's flower
coneflower
salvia
plume poppy
leopard's bane
marigolds

For Fragrance

columbine
dianthus
bee balm
peony
lavender
day lily
lilac
wallflower

viburnum
lilies of the valley
roses
nepeta
garden heliotrope
gardenia
artemesia
southernwood
sweet violets
sweet woodruff

How to Have Longer-Living Cut Flowers

Grandma used to put a few drops of camphorated oil and alcohol in the water with her cut flowers. This simple solution revives fading blossoms and makes flowers last longer.

Today, you can use three drops of the solutions sold for babies' vaporizers, mixed with three drops of rubbing alcohol. Take your fading flowers out of their vase, throw out the old water, add new water with your old-fashioned elixir. Now, before you put your flowers back into the vase, immerse the base of the stems in boiling water to open up their constricted passageways.

Hardy Perennials

Remember that preliminary sketch of your flower beds? Well, now it's time to pick the management team to start filling it in. This team will be made up of flowers that live on year after year. These are called perennials. Grandma used root-hardy perennials as the faithful old family retainers of her flower garden, and you will want to do the same. They will provide your garden with color, design, endurance, economy and improvement. You just plant them and keep them mulched, watered, and trimmed. They will do the rest.

Add to your perennial plantings each year, but don't overplant. Just like people, flowers don't like to spend much time in a crowded place. Give them room to spread out. Many perennials can be divided in autumn at the roots, if they get too crowded. If you live north of New York City, Pittsburgh, Cleveland, Indianapolis, Springfield, or Des Moines, do this in the spring, as the fall-divided roots north of this line may not have a chance to develop properly before winter comes.

Fall Planting

In Grandma Putt's time, spring was the busiest time of the year for folks who lived in the country. The farmers and vegetable gardeners had so much work putting in the spring crops, that they put in incredibly hard days filled with long hours. Any part of the work load that could be moved from this time of the year to a less hectic one, was greatly appreciated; so many healthy, root-hardy perennial plants were put in the ground in the fall, when things slowed down and the autumn harvest was completed. Then, vegetables like asparagus, artichokes, and rhubarb were planted and, along with them, peonies, chrysanthemums, and iris. Dutch bulbs and some of the biennials were also fall-planted.

If you are going into gardening for the first time, I suggest you limit your fall planting the first couple of years to see how well a few individual perennials survive the winter. After the first frost see that they're well mulched to keep winter temperatures constant. If all goes well, plant your root divisions (not seedlings) more heavily the following fall, but keep in mind that Old Man Winter is like a good baseball pitcher. He mixes up his repertoire of tricks every time you come to bat. Be prepared to have him throw you some slow, warm curves as a change of pace follow-up to a good winter that was icy hard and fast. Best fall-planting conditions are a long warm fall, followed by a hard frozen winter. What you don't want is alternate freezes and thawings. It's often better to play it safe and spring-plant, so your perennials develop strong, healthy roots over the long warm growing season.

Spring Planting

You can start your perennials for spring planting indoors in peat pots. These can be set outside as the days become sunny. Then, after the last frost, when the ground begins to get warm, place your flowers in their permanent homes. If everything goes according to plan, they should stay there 'til the cows come home. Feed with garden food (5-10-5 or 4-12- 4) as soon as they're in place, and throw on a half handful several times during the spring and summer. Keeping your plants healthy, sturdy, and well fed will help keep away insects and disease.

SHAMPOOING TIME AGAIN

As I've said many times, bugs don't like soap in their mouths any more than kids so . . . shampoo the foliage of your perennials every other week with a mild soap and water solution. Mix a teaspoon or two of malthion into the solution to eliminate insects.

REMOVE THE BLOOMS

If you don't use many of your perennials for cuttings, be sure to pick off the blooms once they have faded. This prevents the plant from overworking to revive worthless flowering parts.

SPRAYING AND DUSTING

Use the spraying guide in Chapter II to get rid of persistent insect pests and fungus disease. *Please follow directions carefully.*

WATERING

Except for shampooing and insect removal, you should direct your hose toward the feet of perennials. They root deeply, so soak the ground thoroughly in hot, dry weather.

Dividing Perennials

Many of your perennials will prefer to be left alone once they have taken root and become accustomed to their new home. Others, will become overcrowded in a couple of years or more. These, you will have to dig up and root-divide every so often. This simple process will rejuvenate old plants and give you new flowers for planting elsewhere. I *try* to do this about every 3-4 years, depending on how my perennials are growing. Here's how to do it:

1. Dig up the whole plant carefully and wash off the roots and check the crown.

2. Clip off any damaged root fibers.

3. Divide thick-rooted plants (like iris and peony) with a knife. Cut the root into bud-bearing segments and replant.

4. Divide fibrous-rooted plants with your hands. Simply tear the root clump into foliage-bearing segments which you can replant.

5. Divide creeping perennials by cutting away new shoots and replanting them.

Perennial List

Here is a partial list of popular perennial pals to help you select a proper permanent flower-garden picture that meets your needs and suits your tastes:

Low Growing
ajuga
alyssum
arabis
aubretia
cerastium
Christmas rose
chrysanthemum
cup and saucer
dianthus
dicentra
English daisy
hosta
lamium
larpente plumbago
lobelia
lenten rose
myostis

penstemon
polemonium
pulmonaria
shooting star
veronica
violas
yarrow

Medium Growing
achusas
anthemis
bleeding heart
butterfly weed
hardy aster
campanula
catanache
centaurea

cerastium
chrysanthemum
coneflower
coreopsis
coral bells
Shasta daisy
day lily
dicentras
epimedium
feverfew
foxglove
gaillardia
geranium
geum
hibiscus
lorelia
meadow sweet
monk's hood
nepata
phlox
penstemon
evening primrose
shooting star
sunflower
veronica

yarrow

Tall Growing
achusa
hardy aster
centaurea
cimifuga
chrysanthemum
delphinium
doronicum
foxglove
helenium
hibiscus
hollyhock
lupine
lythrum
meadow sweet
meadow rue
monk's hood
peony
penstemon
phlox
physostegia
sunflower
thermopsis

Biennials

Most people see their biennials bloom only once. As you know, these are plants which complete their entire life cycle in two short years. That means they would normally flower only once, the second year after they are planted.

But, it's often quite easy for you to get your biennials to flower during the first year even in the north. Start them indoors, in pots made of peat fiber. Then, plant them in full sun once the ground has warmed to a growing temperature. Biennial buddies include:

> Canterbury bells
> English daisy
> pansies
> foxgloves
> wallflowers
> sweet William
> hollyhocks
> mullien

Shhhh, don't look now . . . but. . . .

Some biennials are self-sowers during the first year. So, you may be happily surprised to see a year-old second-stringer sprouting up just as your two-year-old begins to fade.

Annuals

Each year, the annuals you invite into your garden will become new friends with old familiar names. Petunia, morning glory, and marigold—those names are known so well to most of us it's hard to believe they belong to flowers that grow only a few short months and are gone.

Annuals don't fool around. Their purpose in life is to make seeds. In order to do this, they also make attractive and colorful flowers which provide you and me with garden beauty from the last spring frost to the first one in the fall. They are very easy to grow being disease, drought, and heat resistant. They come in all colors and sizes. They are inexpensive and available in seed packets or as seedlings in nursery flats.

I prefer the seedlings myself, but my girls love to grow flowers from seed. Each year, I let them use the old bulb bed as soon as the daffodils and tulips are through with it. The girls have the best luck growing zinnias from seed.

Three Main Groups

Annuals can be put into three convenient groups or categories which will help make it easy for you to choose which ones will do best in your garden. These are hardy annuals, half-hardy annuals, and tender annuals.

Hardy annuals like sweet peas, pansies, poppies, and love-in-a-mist may be sown as seed late in the fall. These will bloom earliest in the spring.

The half-hardy annuals include marigolds, petunias, lupines, and zinnias. These will take fall sowing if you live in California or the border states (Kentucky, Tennessee, etc.). I usually plant both these cold-resistant types from flats in the spring. This way, they can be put in the ground right after the last spring frost. My advice is for you not to risk an entire planting to the whims of Old Man Winter. If you must plant in the fall; plant only half your flowers. Then you can hedge your over-wintering bet with another half crop in the spring. Seeds are cheap, but there's something psychologically damaging about losing an entire planting before you're halfway into spring!

Winter Mulching

If you do plant some of these flowers for over the winter, cover them with a very loose mulch made up of straw, pine needles, or shredded shrubbery prunings.

The tender annuals like begonias, China asters, dahlias, gourds, morning glories, and stocks make up the bulk of all annual flowers. Most of these are native to countries, and regions of this country, which have long warm growing seasons. It's almost always best to let your nurseryman start these indoors for you to plant from flats when the ground is warm enough in your area to permit continued growth.

Back to Your Plan Before You Buy

Now, before you rush ahead and buy whatever annuals strike your fancy at the nursery or garden center, go back to that preliminary sketch you made of your garden. Ask yourself if the annuals you are thinking about will fit in with the bulbs, biennials and perennials already there. Will they harmonize as to size, shape, and color with your other flowers? Will they bloom quickly enough to augment early garden color, or take up the slack when your bulbs or early blooming perennials begin to fade? Does the available garden space available for them have any special soil or shade problems?

Once you have determined the answers to all these questions, go ahead and purchase what you need. If you buy from seed, remember that a little bit will go a long way. Don't oversow. It's usually best to buy both seeds and seedlings by name. Seed mixtures, especially, are often not very reliable in producing the shapes, color, and varieties you want most. Check the age of the seed and the germination percentages on the packets.

One more mild warning: annuals often grow differently in different local soil conditions. If your soil is extremely fertile, consider named types and varieties (especially dwarfs) from reliable firms which promise to grow true.

Planting and Culture of Annuals

Prepare your annual flower beds as you would for tulips or perennials. These flowers are less choosy than most but why not give them a treat? The less work they have in rooting and feeding themselves, the more time they will have to produce flowers.

For a hundred-square-foot annual bed, blend the following ingredients with the soil already there: 100 pounds of peat moss, 50 pounds of gypsum, 25 pounds of garden food, and 6 bushels of well-rotted compost or processed sewerage sludge. Once this mixture is well-blended, rake and level the entire area.

More than likely though, you will not plant your annuals separately from your longer lasting flowering plants. Old-timers, like perennials, relish meeting new friends and working with them to please you.

After sowing the seed, mulch with newspapers. Remove the papers *immediately* when the seeds begin to sprout.

After sprouting is going well, a low mulch will keep the ground moist and prevent weed growth. Pull out any weeds by hand and apply a preemergent weed killer.

Feed these flowers as you would perennials and bulbs. They need energy and growth-power. I feed my flowers with a handful of garden food about once every three weeks. Their idea of a special treat is fish meal. (To each his own, I always say). Throw some of that on from time to time to show them you care.

These beauties prefer to wash their own foliage in the rain. When it's dry you can water them with a watering can or a soaker-hose. Wet the ground at their feet.

The tried-and-true liquid soap and water shampoo once a month will ward off bugs and most disease problems before they have a chance to get started.

THINNING, CUTTING BACK AND PINCHING OFF

Thinning is a very important step in growing annuals. Be as strong-minded in thinning annuals as you are with strawberries. Otherwise, they will crowd each other out and inhibit growth (or prevent it entirely). Pull out all but the hardiest. You'll be glad you did this when you see the survivors bloom big, strong, and long.

Cutting back is also good for these flowers. Allow them to bloom once. Then, the second blooms can be cut. This will encourage more and bigger blooms later.

Pinching off is another important operation in the care and culture of annuals. If you pinch off faded blooms, your flowers will repay you with new and vigorous growth.

SUCCESSION SOWINGS

To keep up a constant supply of fast-growing annuals like petunias, etc., sow several times during the season. You will have blooms until fall.

The following lists should meet all your annual growing needs:

For Borders
ageratum
alyssum
balsam
bells of Ireland
marigold
nicotiana
petunia
salvia farinacea and
    splendens
centaurea
cleome
cosmos
cynoglossum
larkspur
snapdragon
statice
zinnia

For the Seaside
alyssum
dusty miller
hollyhock
statice
lupine
petunia

279

For Window Boxes
alyssum
begonia semperflorens
coleus
lobelia
nierembergia
cascade petunias
thunbergia

For Foliage
amaranthus
basil
canna
castor bean
coleus
dusty miller
kochia
perilla

For Partial Shade
balsam
begonia
browallia
calendula
coleus
impatiens
lobelia
myosotis
nicotiana
pansy
salvia
torenia

For Cutting
asters
bells of Ireland
carnation
celosia
centaurea (bachelor
  buttons)
cosmos
cynoglossum
dahlia
daisy, Tahoka
gaillardia
gerbera
gomphrena
larkspur
marigold
nasturtium
petunias
rudbeckia
salpiglossis
salvia
scabiosa
snapdragons
statice
verbena
zinnia

For Drying
baby's breath
bells of Ireland
celosia
cornflower

everlasting
gaillardia
marigold
petunia
phlox
stock
sunflower
sweet alyssum
sweet pea
verbena
zinnia

Medium Growers
balsam 15″
basil 15″
bells of Ireland 24″
carnation 15-20″
celosia (medium cristata
  types such as fireglow)
  20-24″
cynoglossum 18″
dahlia (such as Unwin's
  Dwarf Mix) 20-24″
dusty miller 12-24″
  (Centaurea gymnocarpa)
gaillardia 24-30″
gomphrena 18″
helichrysum 24-30″
impatiens 15-18″
nicotiana 12-24″
petunias 12-15″
rudbeckia 16-18″

salpiglossis 20-30″
salvia 18-30″
snapdragons 15-24″
  (Vacationland, Hit Parade,
  Sprites) 12-15″
  (Knee High) 12-15″
verbena 12-24″
zinnia 18-30″

Tall Growers
amaranthus 3-4′
asters 36″
celosia (tall plumosa sorts
  such as Forest Fire) 30-48″
centaurea (bachelor buttons)
  30″
cleome 3-4′
cosmos 3′
dahlia (such as cactus and
  giant flowered types)
  30-48″
hollyhock 4-5′
larkspur 2-3′
marigolds 30-36″
ricinus (castor bean) 8-10′
scabiosa 2-3′
statice 30″
snapdragons (Rockets)
  30-36″
zinnia 30-36″

Ground Covers
cobaea
creeping zinnia
  (Sanvitalia procumbens)
lobelia
mesembryanthemum
morning glory
myosotis
nasturtium
nierembergia
portulaca
sweet alyssum
sweet pea
thunbergia
verbena
vinca

In Rock Gardens
alyssum
candytuft
gazania
mesembryanthemum
pansy
verbena
plus ground covers

For Edging: 3-18"
ageratum 6-12"
alyssum 4-6"
begonia 4-12"

calendula 12"
candytuft 8"
centaurea (dwarf bachelor
  buttons) 10-12"
celosia (dwarf, such as Fiery
  Feather or Jewel Box)
  4-12"
coleus 12-15"
dianthus 12"
dusty miller (such as *Centaurea
  Candidissima and Cineraria
  Maritima* Diamond) 6-10"
gazania 8"
gomphrena 9"
heliotrope 12-15"
impatiens 6-8"
lobelia 8"
mesembryanthemum 6"
myosotis 12"
nierembergia 6"
phlox 7-15"
pansy 6-8"
petunia 12-15"
portulaca 4-6"
snapdragon (Floral Carpet)
  6-8"
torenia 8-12"
verbena 8-12"
vinca 10"
zinnia, dwarf 6-12"

Roses

Raising flowers can be a casual pastime or a time-consuming art. This is most especially true of roses, and either aim has its own rewards.

If you have plans to raise roses for the thrill of developing a new variety that will win you first prize at the national rose show, I suggest you pay your dues by reading some of the very sophisticated and worthwhile literature on rose cultivation.

If, on the other hand, you want to grow a variety of roses for their regal beauty and delightful fragrance, read on.

An Old, Old Story

The first roses may well have been growing in that First Garden. If so, Eve should have been more like my wife who, I find, will take much more interest in a bouquet of roses than in a basket of fruit!

The roses we grow today seem to stem from Asia and those early Bible lands. In the West, they have been traced definitely as far back as the Bronze Age civilization on Crete, nearly 6,000 years ago. (*Flower Chronicles,* B. Hollingsworth Rutgers University Press.)

However, there are at least a hundred species and varieties growing wild in many northern countries including our own.

Enterprising gardeners have carried cultivated species of roses wherever they have traveled and lived . . . from Australia to hell-and-gone.

Today, there are 5,000 or so cultivated rose varieties with more being developed every year. So, I think it's safe to say that the rose is, both historically and currently, the universal garden flower.

In Grandma's day, folks had lots of room, so most homes were planted with at least a modest rose garden. June was the month when roses seemed to be everywhere within reach of your senses.

Almost all roses have a delightful fragrance and flavor, in addition to blooms beyond compare (unless compared with other roses). Grandma Putt took advantage of these qualities by using rose petals in sachets, potpourris, salads, and teas. In addition, she made rose wine and rose-hip jelly. Rose hips, the fruit of the rose plant, are very rich in nutrients, especially vitamin C.

Today, even if you can't promise yourself a rose garden, you can grow roses and get more for your money. Modern roses bloom for a second season in the fall. So, why not learn a few of the simple facts and techniques that will help you grow your own?

Telling Them Apart

Roses are identified by the way they grow and by their structure. Basically, they are bush-type, climbing plants, shrub plants, and tree plants. The bush-type plants are the most commonly grown. Among them are hybrid teas, grandifloras, floribundas, polyantha, hybrid polyantha, hybrid perpetual, and miniature roses.

Hybrid tea roses are the most popularly raised. They are grown for their long stems and giant blooms. They are fast growers and will easily reach a height of three feet and a width of four feet, in one season. If the lady of your house is a student of flower arranging, or a lover of cut flowers, these are for you. Included in this class is Peace, the world's most popular rose.

Grandifloras are the newest rose classification, produced from crosses of floribunda and hybrid tea roses. They are becoming more and more popular every year. If you like big blooms, these are just your meat. They grow tall and make a good background for your rose garden . . . or for any garden. I have seen these used as property dividers and the effect is stunning. They are the easiest rose to care for and grow.

Floribunda is just what the name "flowering abundance" implies, and comes from crosses of tea roses and polyantha. This rose gives the hybrid tea a real run for its money in the popularity race, because of its numerous flowers. The blooms are arranged in large clusters. They make a good foreground, planted along hedges or in front of hybrid teas in the rose garden. I like them best for group plantings. The famous Sweetheart rose is a floribunda.

Polyantha roses are the baby ramblers you see used for edgings. The flowers are small, but appear in clusters.

Hybrid polyantha is very similar to the floribunda. Some day, I expect to see these two groups merged. Until then, tuck the information away in your mind and substitute one for the other whenever the occasion arises.

Hybrid perpetuals are the roses that Grandma grew, and probably her grandmother before her. The famous American Beauty rose was one of these (still is, for that matter). These were the June roses that brightened the summer days of early settlers. Grandma's favorites were red General Jacks. They are not so commonly grown in modern gardens because of its one flowering season.

Miniature roses can have a hundred uses in your landscape plans. They seem to always be in bloom from spring to fall. They grow from twelve to eighteen inches tall and can be used in borders, or as single specimens.

Climbing roses are the roses that leave a strong imprint on most peoples' memories. That's because they appear in masses of color. Most of these are June roses. Included in this group are the pillar, ramblers, and even some new, ever-blooming varieties. They make an excellent boundary plant and serve as a perfect cover for an ugly wall or fence. Who can't at least picture in his mind the climbing roses that covered the trellises and arched the doorways of those romantic cottages that now cost too much to rent? Climbers have heavy canes that need staking or some other support. Ramblers have thinner, more flexible canes. They're great for walls. Pillars don't grow as high as climbers. They're trained on poles and pillars.

Trailing roses are an offshoot of the climbers. Often called ground-cover roses, these trailing types can form huge mats and mounds.

Tree roses are an exception to the rule that "only God can make a tree." Any bush-type rose and even some climbers, can be grafted to tree stock. The trunks are commonly four feet tall and the flowering top part bushes out as far as its ground growing cousins. In the late fall, the roses should be protected. One way to do this is to pound some stakes into the ground and make a cylinder of black plastic sheeting around them. Fill this cylinder to the very top with leaves. Pot-grown specimens can be brought into a dark, moist, cold-storage area or root cellar.

Shrub roses are descendants of the original wild rose. They are hardy and well worth cultivating in your garden. Among these shrub or species roses you will find: multiflora, cabbage, Memorial, Father Hugo's, rugosa, alba, crested moss, hermosa, old blush, Nevada, old pink moss and the American Harrison's yellow.

Grandma grew several including: old pink mosses, white Bourbon, and damask roses (for fragrance).

Planting and Growing Procedures

Roses are not only beautiful, they are among the easiest plants to grow. Give this Royal Mistress lots of fresh air, sunshine, food, and water and you should have no problems.

These are the good cultural practices so important to growing success. If you handle these practices in a sound common-sense and regular way, you will have beautiful roses.

SELECTION AND PLANTING

You can purchase canned or potted roses or dry-root varieties. The dry-root roses are usually two-year-old budded stock which is dormant. These plants are graded 1, 2, and 3. If possible, buy first-grade stock. Plant canned and potted roses in the spring after all danger of frost is past. Plant dry-root roses in the fall or, where extremely cold winters are the rule, in the spring.

Your soil should be worked deeply. Fertile, loose, well-drained soil in a sunny spot. Roses need eight to twelve hours of sun a day. If your soil doesn't stack up as good enough for a large rose bed, add five pounds of rose food or mild garden food to the soil surface. Then, mix in fifty pounds of peat, twenty-five pounds of gypsum, and three bushels of 60-40 gravel. All of this goes into a hundred-square-foot area. Mix this planting soil well and deeply.

Grandma's roses had been growing in place for years by the time I lived there, but I have planted thousands of roses since. The best time to plant them is in the fall or spring when you can get a spade in the ground. Plant them the same day you bring them home. That's important so I'll repeat it . . . *plant them the same day you bring them home!*

Plant potted roses in a hole that's wide enough and deep enough to allow their roots to spread and be comfortable.

A ROSE GROWING TIP FROM GRANDMA

Grandma Putt told her gardening friends to add a half cup of epsom salts to the soil surface of newly planted roses. This is still good advice, as the salts promote richer color, thicker petals and stronger roots. Now, talk to your rose . . . welcome her to her new home.

Feed your roses once a month if they are everblooming varieties. Old-fashioned "June" roses only should be fed in the spring.

As I described in *Plants Are Like People,* you can feed and water roses in the same operation. Do this by planting a large fruit-juice can that's open at both ends between each rose. Fill these cans halfway to the top with pea pebbles and, from time to time, add a small amount of food to the can. When you water deeply, this food will soak down to root level where it's most needed.

Put down a thick mulch of cedar chips between your roses to keep their feet moist and weeds down. Use preemerge weed killers to keep you off your knees.

Set your potted plants in a hole that's big enough and deep enough to let the roots stretch out. Fill the hole to the top with water and let it drain off naturally before putting Miss Rose in her new home.

In the case of dry-root roses, soak the roots in water or cover with wet burlap. Cut off any dead or damaged parts. Don't bury your rose. The hole needs only to be wide and deep enough to give the roots plenty of growing space.

Place a mound of soil in the bottom and spread out the roots. Now, begin to refill, pushing the soil down firmly. When your hole is half full of soil, fill the remainder with water and allow to drain, next fill the remainder of the hole with soil. Be sure that the bulge or graft union ends up two inches below the surface. This is important if you want to raise grafted stock instead of first-root stock.

Now that the rose is planted, put a small wall of soil around the outside perimeter of the hole to hold water. Water deeply. If it's spring, cut the canes back to a half-foot.

Make cuts above the outside bud. In fall, leave canes alone. Cover the entire plant with a light soil mixture and allow to set for ten days.

When you pick or cut roses, be sure to leave one healthy five-leaf cluster on the stem. Leaving this good leaf will permit future growth from the same cane.

Grandma talked to and cared for her own roses . . . they were her pride and joy. She made a regular practice of pinching off side buds on her hybrid teas to promote big, healthy blooms from the leading buds. Also, she never let faded blooms hang on her roses. I suggest you pick these off as soon as you see them. She shampooed them once a month and grew chives and garlic at their feet to ward off aphids and other pests.

If you have insect or fungus problems, check the USDA approved list of controls in Chapter II. Remove diseased parts of roses and spray as directed to prevent future damage from the same source.

There are thousands of varieties of roses . . . far too many to list here. Here are a dozen outstanding beauties selected by my beautiful friend and fellow rose enthusiast, Dinah Shore:

Hybrid Teas
Americana
American Heritage
John F. Kennedy
Peace

Floribunda
Sutter's Gold
White Queen

Grandiflora
Camelot
Comanche

Climbers
Don Juan
Imperial Blaze
White Dawn

Old-Fashioned
Harrison's Yellow

I hope growing roses is easy, fun and as worthwhile for you as it was for Grandma Putt, and still is for Ilene and me.

May the first rose you see each spring bring you joy, and the last rose of autumn bring you peace.

Epilogue:
When all Else Fails...
Plant a Tree

There is much that I wanted to include in this book that I have of necessity had to leave out. For that, I sincerely apologize.

Looking at what I have just written, I am sure that many of my fond memories of hoeing, weeding, and working in the garden at my Grandmother Puttnam's, have grown "fonder" in retrospect than they may have been at the moment. . . . I suppose there is something about small boys that makes them begrudge even the happiest of tasks, and yearn to go a-wandering. If I seem to have gathered more "knowledge" and satisfaction in looking back toward her garden, than I actually gained and used on the spot . . . for this I apologize also (but to her).

And if, in reliving some of the garden highlights of that year, I move you to try and you *fail* to become a successful gardener . . . for that I will hang my head in shame!

Grandma Putt once had some words of advice for a friend of hers who had no apparent knack for growing things. "When all else fails," she said, "plant a tree."

I hope that you of the black-thumb clan will take her advice and plant a kind old shady oak or maple or elm . . . and call it by your own name. Then, each year, it will grow in strength as you will grow in wisdom. Perhaps, one day, sitting beneath the branches of your tree, you will suddenly look up and realize it is a living testimonial to your gardening know-how . . . for this I will say, "You're welcome!"

JERRY BAKER 1972

Index

297